STUDENT UNIT G

AS History
UNIT 1

Module 2582:
Nazi Germany, 1933–45

Patrick Flood

Series Editor: Derrick Murphy

Philip Allan Updates
Market Place
Deddington
Oxfordshire
OX15 0SE

tel: 01869 338652
fax: 01869 337590
e-mail: sales@philipallan.co.uk
www.philipallan.co.uk

© Philip Allan Updates 2001
Revised February 2002

ISBN-13: 978-0-86003-482-7
ISBN-10: 0-86003-482-8

All rights reserved; no part of this publication may be reproduced, stored in a retrieval system, or transmitted, in any form or by any means, electronic, mechanical, photocopying, recording or otherwise without either the prior written permission of Philip Allan Updates or a licence permitting restricted copying in the United Kingdom issued by the Copyright Licensing Agency Ltd, 90 Tottenham Court Road, London W1T 4LP.

This Guide has been written specifically to support students preparing for the OCR History Unit 1 examination. The content has been neither approved nor endorsed by OCR and remains the sole responsibility of the author.

Printed by Information Press, Eynsham, Oxford

Contents

Introduction 4

■ ■ ■

Content Guidance

About this section 8

The establishment and consolidation of Nazi authority

Hitler's political aims 9
Hitler's position, January–February 1933 9
From Chancellor to Führer, January 1933–August 1934 11
Nazism: was Hitler 'master in the Third Reich' or 'weak dictator'? 16
Führer power: theory and practice 17
The role of the SS and the police state 19
Himmler and the SS 20

The popularity of Hitler and the Nazis

Basic assumptions of Nazi propaganda 22
Hitler's personal popularity 24
Dissent, opposition and resistance in the Third Reich 25

The persecution of the Jews

The *Volksgemeinschaft* 30
Anti-Semitism in Nazi ideology 30
The genesis of the Holocaust 31
The main stages of persecution, 1933–39 32

■ ■ ■

Questions and Answers

About this section 36
Q1 The consolidation of Hitler's power 37
Q2 The Nazi system of government 43
Q3 Opposition to Hitler 49
Q4 Nazi anti-Semitism 55

AS History

Introduction

About this guide

This guide has been written for students preparing for the OCR Module 2582, Option 5.1.3.7, 'Nazi Germany, 1933–45'. It is a *guide* rather than a textbook, and aims to familiarise you with the essential detail needed to tackle the exam, the types of question you will be asked, the format of the exam and what the examiners will be looking for.

The second section of the guide, **Content Guidance**, gives a broad overview of the option. In the short space available, much detail has had to be omitted. Students are advised to use a good basic textbook on Nazi Germany. There are a number of these available. Since the option is a document-based paper, students should familiarise themselves with some of the main documents on the various topics. By far the best collection of documents on Nazi Germany in English can be found in G. Pridham and J. Noakes (eds) (2000) *Nazism*, Vols 1, 2 and 3, University of Exeter Press.

In the third section, **Questions and Answers**, there are four examples of examination questions. Each question consists of three sub-questions on various topics within the option. The questions are followed by examiners' mark schemes, which state what examiners are looking for. In response to each of the three questions there is a worked answer that would score in the A-grade range. For the last question a C-grade response is also given.

The examiner's comments on the answers to each sub-question aim to help you see how the examiner is thinking.

The format of the option and examination

The examination at the end of this option is 1 hour long. It is important to remember that it is a *source-based paper*. You are given four passages on the relevant theme within the option. The passages are normally *primary* sources. The total word length of the four passages does not normally exceed 400 words. Sometimes there might be a pictorial source — a cartoon or a photograph.

The total mark for the option is 120. There are three sub-questions on the given passages, in ascending order of difficulty and mark allocation.

Sub-question (a) carries 20 marks. You are asked to refer to one of the passages and explain or define the meaning of a word or phrase within that passage. The objective of the question is to test 'comprehension of a source'.

Sub-question (b) carries 40 marks and asks you to look at two of the passages. The objective is 'comparison of two sources'. You will be expected to point out how the sources differ, and, where relevant, how they agree.

OCR Unit 1

Sub-question (c) carries 60 marks. Here, you are asked to consider *all* the passages in your answer. You will be given a statement, a proposition or assertion, which you should then test against the information and evidence in the passages and against knowledge of your own.

The questions are progressive, so you should answer sub-questions (a) and (b) before tackling (c).

There are no prescribed documents. Those chosen for the examination will be fairly central, relating to the themes in the content of the option. The aim is to emphasise various skills over a range of documents.

The *quality* of the answers is more important than the quantity. However, as a rough guide, bearing in mind the fairly short amount of time for the exam, answers to sub-question (a) might be expected to occupy around half a side of A4 exam paper. Question (b), carrying 40 marks, should be around one side long and question (c), a mini-essay, should occupy around two to two and a half sides. Because the final question, (c), carries half the total marks, it should occupy around half the writing time, say 30 minutes.

What the examiners are looking for

It is essential to remember that on all sub-questions you are expected to use your own contextual knowledge. Much information can be gleaned from the given extracts, but those who merely paraphrase the extracts without using their knowledge of the topic will not normally rise above half marks, no matter how sophisticated the paraphrasing is. Those who display good knowledge and understanding of the topic and combine this with an intelligent reading of the passages should achieve A or B grades. It should be possible to gain a C grade without high powers of analysis or evaluation of the passages, but to be in this category you would be expected to show some outside knowledge.

Since the passages will usually be primary sources, you will not be tested on the historiography of the topics. This is a source-based paper testing contextual knowledge and evaluation of sources.

Sub-question (a) will specifically invite you to use your own knowledge to define or explain a word or phrase in the given passage. Clearly, some guidance and help will be given by the specific passage, and you should read the other passages to see if there is any help there. Relevant cross-referencing is not essential, but in certain cases it might be useful in answering sub-question (a).

On sub-question (b), testing the comparison of two sources, it is tempting and all too easy simply to indulge in a detailed paraphrasing of the two sources, especially when they are saying obviously different things. Even a very detailed paraphrasing will only result in a low C mark, at best. The question requires you to apply your own (hopefully detailed) knowledge of the topic under consideration and to explain not just where the sources differ, but *why* they differ. Good answers should also point out where the sources agree, where relevant. The sub-question will not always be phrased in a straightforward fashion. Occasionally you might be asked to consider the extent to which Source X supports Source Y, for example. Questions of date, author, purpose and audience are important here.

Sub-question (c) requires a mini-essay. The statement in the question is an assertion with which you may agree or disagree (usually the former). It is tempting on this question simply to write a *general* answer, without referring to the given passages. No matter how good your answer might be in terms of focus and analysis, this type of answer will not score above a low C grade. You should remember that this is a *document-based* option and you are expected to use the given passages at all times. What is required is a sharp focus on the title in the question, sound analysis and reference to all four passages in the context of the question. To score highly, references to passages should go beyond basic statements like 'as Source A says…'. Similarly, answers that simply paraphrase all the passages without really addressing the question or offering any analysis will attain a D or low C grade. Clearly, the examiners are looking for a *combination* of knowledge, focus, analysis and relevant reference to passages. One possible approach would be to use reference to passages to illustrate or support the point being made.

On all three sub-questions, quotation from the passages is encouraged, but only where it is relevant to the question.

This option is concerned with the domestic policies of Nazi Germany. Nazi foreign policy aims and actions should be considered only in so far as they affected the consolidation and popularity of Nazi rule. After studying this option, you should have an awareness and understanding of:
- Hitler's aims and methods
- how and why Hitler and the Nazis were able to establish and consolidate their rule
- how the Nazi political system operated
- the nature of the SS police state
- the popularity of the regime and the forms of resistance to it

The extent to which the Nazis were able to succeed in their aims will be assessed by a study of the ways in which German society was transformed between 1933 and 1939 and, in particular, the implementation of Nazi racial policies in Germany and eastern Europe.

To aid study, in this section the content outlined above is broken down into three parts:
(1) The establishment and consolidation of Nazi authority (page 9).
(2) The popularity of Hitler and the Nazis (page 22).
(3) The persecution of the Jews (page 29).

At every stage, you must bear in mind the ways in which the units are linked with each other.

The establishment and consolidation of Nazi authority

The focus in this part of the option is on the period following Hitler's appointment as Chancellor in 1933, but students should understand the main features of the Nazis' political aims and have an awareness of the comparative weakness of Hitler's position at the time of his appointment.

Hitler's political aims

The basis of Hitler's political aims and methods can be found in a speech he made before the Supreme Court at Leipzig in September 1930. Called as a witness at the trial of three Army officers accused of working for the Nazis, he said:

> The National Socialist movement will try to achieve its aim with constitutional means in this state. The constitution provides only the methods, not the aim. In this constitutional way we shall try to gain decisive majorities in the legislative bodies so that the moment we succeed we can give the state the form that corresponds to our ideas.

The Nazis, therefore, would use the democratic process of the despised Weimar constitution in order to achieve power. Once in power they would work rapidly and progressively to destroy liberal democracy and establish what many historians regard as a totalitarian dictatorship. The extent to which this was actually achieved is assessed on pages 11–19, but there is little doubt that Hitler had political aims that can broadly be described as totalitarian. Essentially this entailed the following:

- the establishment of a one-party state
- the elimination of all institutions and organisations that allowed independent thought
- rigid censorship of the media and all forms of 'culture'
- 'mobilisation' of society through propaganda against all common enemies
- 'Nazification' or 'coordination' of important institutions like the armed forces, civil service, trade unions, education system, police forces and, if possible, the churches

These can be seen as broad and general aims, but it is important to realise that Hitler had no specific plan or 'timetable' for their implementation. Although he was appointed Chancellor on 30 January 1933, he was as yet a long way from achieving absolute power.

Hitler's position, January–February 1933

Hitler was appointed at a time when the Nazi vote was declining. Between July and November 1932 the Nazi Party (NSDAP) lost some 2 million votes and 34 Reichstag seats while the communist (KPD) vote continued to rise. However, the NSDAP was still the largest party in the Reichstag. Hitler's bargaining position with President Hindenburg and former Chancellor Franz von Papen was, if anything, weaker in January 1933 than it had been in August 1932 when, with the Nazis holding 230 seats in the Reichstag, Hitler had failed to gain the chancellorship. In 1933 Hitler was effectively 'rescued' by the members of the conservative élites and 'invited' to power when his fortunes seemed to be declining. In the historian Alan Bullock's famous words, he was 'jobbed into power by a backstairs intrigue'.

However, with a growing fear of a communist or even a Nazi SA (stormtrooper) uprising, Hitler was the only candidate who could claim to represent the forces of the right in German politics. There was no alternative other than a military dictatorship, which was ruled out by Hindenburg. Although Hitler was head of government, Hindenburg was still head of state. Hitler had been appointed by Hindenburg entirely legitimately under the terms of the Weimar Constitution. With Hindenburg's friend von Papen acting as Vice-Chancellor, Hitler could, it was thought, be 'boxed in'.

Hitler was one of only three Nazis in the 12-man Cabinet. However, the other two Nazis, Goering and Frick, held the important posts of Prussian Minister of the Interior and Reich Minister of the Interior, respectively. The administration of the police in the dominant state of Prussia was effectively in the hands of the Nazis.

In order to maintain a majority in the Reichstag, the Nazis would have to form a coalition with the Nationalists. Clearly, this was an impediment for Hitler. An important condition of Hitler's, agreed in the negotiations leading to his appointment, was that the Reichstag should be dissolved and new elections immediately declared, with the aim of achieving at least the necessary two-thirds majority in order to change the constitution 'legally', and effectively bypass the Reichstag.

Hitler's ultimate aim was to combine and then abolish the positions of President and Chancellor, and rule as the Führer of a one-party state. Hindenburg, the representative and figurehead of the social, political and military élites which had dominated imperial Germany, would, as long as he continued to be President, be the obstacle to the achievement of total power.

It was vital at this stage for Hitler to cultivate an image of 'respectability' at home and abroad. Owing his very position as Chancellor to the forces of law and order and traditional conservatism, he had to tread carefully to avoid alienating the conservative politicians, leaders of big business, the civil service and the armed forces. He had to 'court' the German establishment. The rabble-rousing 'drummer of the masses' had now to appear to be the responsible statesman.

Hitler's fundamental problem in the early days of power was how to balance the interests of the traditional élites with those of the SA — the brown-shirted stormtroopers, the Nazi Party's private army. The number of stormtroopers had swollen dramatically during the years of the Depression and some estimates put membership at approaching 3 million by 1933. The SA had played a very important role in the NSDAP's decisive election breakthrough after 1929, but was feared and despised by the forces of the establishment as an unruly, violent mob. Indeed, conservatives, senior civil servants, captains of industry and senior Army officers — the very groups that Hitler needed for consolidation of his power — made very little distinction between the stormtroopers and the communists. The outbreaks of SA street violence that followed Hitler's appointment — the beatings up of Jews and socialists and communists — only served to increase these fears. Hitler had a major problem on his hands, which was not to be resolved until the purging of the SA leadership in the Night of the Long Knives in the summer of 1934.

From Chancellor to Führer, January 1933–August 1934

In the extraordinarily short period of 18 months, by semi-legal measures, complicity, terror and intimidation, Hitler became Führer, a position in which he could exercise, in theory, unrestrained and unlimited power. This period began with the Reichstag election campaign, culminating on 5 March, and ended with the removal of the influence of forces that could possibly challenge Hitler: the conservative élites and the brown-shirted stormtroopers.

The consolidation of the Nazi dictatorship

Various stages and events mark the consolidation of the Nazi dictatorship during 1933:

- **Appeal to the German People** (31 January)
  This projected the image of a national uprising. Despite the vagueness of the message, the emphasis of the appeal was on the feebleness and divisiveness of Weimar democracy. The economic and spiritual regeneration of German society was promised and only Hitler and the Nazis, it was claimed, could save the nation from economic ruin, class warfare and disintegration. Naturally, the German Communist Party, the KPD, was singled out as the main enemy. It was a manifesto cleverly designed to appeal to all the forces of social and political conservatism, but designed also to distance the Nazis from the traditional message of the Nationalist Party.

- **Decree for the Protection of the German People** (4 February)
  This was imposed for the duration of the election campaign. Ostensibly a measure to combat communist 'terrorist' activities, it provided for restrictions of press freedom and 'protective custody' of offenders, the latter becoming a euphemism for acts of terror carried out by the Nazi regime later in the 1930s.

- **Reichstag Fire Decree** (28 February)
  On 27 February the Reichstag building was set on fire and a young Dutch communist, van der Lubbe, was found acting suspiciously. Whether this was a

genuine communist attempt or not, it came at a very convenient time for the Nazis, in the middle of an election campaign in which the 'communist threat' was the fundamental theme. It was good propaganda for the Nazis and, more importantly, could be used to justify the arrests of political opponents. Within hours, the Decree of the Reich President for the Protection of People and State was issued. This provided for restrictions on personal liberty, on the right of free expression of opinion and of the press and freedom of assembly and association. Warrants for house searches, confiscations and restrictions on property rights were permissible 'beyond the legal limits otherwise prescribed'. The justification was that there was a 'state of emergency' and by implication the decree would be repealed once the 'emergency' was over. In fact, it was never repealed and lasted for the duration of the Third Reich. Effectively, the Reichstag Fire Decree provided the semi-legal basis for the Nazi dictatorship and rule by terror.

- **Day of Potsdam** (21 March)
  The day before the establishment of Dachau concentration camp (see below), the more respectable side of the regime was displayed in the Day of Potsdam. This was a deliberate attempt to appeal to the forces of traditional Prussian conservatism, which had dominated imperial Germany and maintained power and influences in the armed forces, civil service and judiciary throughout the Weimar period. Here at Potsdam, the training ground of the Kaiser's military élite, was the old Field Marshal Hindenburg in his full military uniform, representing the forces of Prussian junkerdom and Germany's glorious past, placed side-by-side with Hitler, dressed in a suit, representing Germany's potentially glorious future. The occasion, ostensibly to mark the opening of the new Reichstag, was a masterstroke by Hitler's new Propaganda Minister, Goebbels. The theme, though unsubtle, was effective. Hitler simultaneously represented continuity with the past and radical policies for the future.

- **Dachau concentration camp** (22 March)
  Beneath the cloak of legality, a wave of terror and repression was sweeping through Germany. In Bavaria alone, some 10,000 communists and socialists had been arrested and taken into so-called 'protective custody'. A few miles from Munich, outside the town of Dachau, a former warehouse was established as a concentration camp on 22 March. It was publicly advertised as a 'deterrent' and a 'correction centre' for members of the KPD and SPD. Although rumours of the brutalities inflicted on the inmates quickly spread, the initial targeting of those on the political left appeared to conform well with the propaganda myth of the national uprising.

- **Enabling Law** (23 March)
  Hitler wanted an enabling law so that the government could introduce laws without Reichstag approval over the next 4 years. This would emasculate the Reichstag and effectively destroy the Weimar Constitution and parliamentary democracy.

  In order to proceed legally, Hitler needed a two-thirds majority to amend the constitution, hence the elections on 5 March. The results were a great disappointment to Hitler. After weeks of Nazi government, less than 44% of the electorate had voted for the Nazis and even by forming a coalition with the Nationalists, the Nazis could only command 51% of the seats in the Reichstag, well short of the target. The 94 members of the socialist SPD could not be expected to vote for Hitler's enabling bill and so could be discounted. The KPD deputies were banned under the Reichstag Fire Decree and the Nationalists were coalition partners. This just left the Catholic Centre Party.

On the day of the passage of the bill, Hitler promised to respect the rights of Catholics and the Catholic Church. There were areas of common ground between the Church and the Nazis, such as fear of communism, theological anti-Semitism and anti-feminism. The Centre Party also felt helpless and feared reprisals if they didn't vote with the Nazis. As a result, the Enabling Law was passed by 444 votes to the 94 of the SPD. All laws would now be drafted by the Chancellor and come into operation on the day of publication. The signature of President Hindenburg was no longer needed for the issuing of decrees and the Reichstag became a mere cipher of the Nazi government. Importantly, what was in effect the destruction of Weimar democracy was given the appearance of legality.

- **Law Against the Establishment of Parties** (14 July)
  After the passing of the Enabling Law the banning of parties other than the Nazis became only a matter of time. The KPD was already banned as an illegal organisation. The SPD was officially banned on 22 June after reports of anti-Nazi activities by exiles abroad. The Nationalists, no longer needed as coalition partners, disbanded, and on 5 July the formerly influential Catholic Centre Party followed suit. Still wrestling with the dilemma of whether to cooperate with the Nazi regime, the party virtually had the ground cut from under its feet by the concordat between the papacy and the Nazi regime signed on 8 July. The one-party state was formally established on 14 July 1933 by the Law Against the Establishment of Parties, less than 6 months after Hitler had been 'jobbed into power'.

The policy of *Gleichschaltung*

Translated into English, *Gleichschaltung* means 'putting into the same gear'. A more suitable expression is 'forcible coordination'. All institutions or organisations which could possibly rival or challenge the Nazi dictatorship had to be either eliminated or Nazified. The Law Against the Establishment of Parties can be seen as part of this process. *Gleichschaltung* was carried out more effectively in some areas than others. The armed forces and churches were never fully coordinated. As will be seen in the next area of focus ('The popularity of Hitler and the Nazis', pages 22–29), it is no coincidence that the only serious opposition to the regime came from these two groupings. The following were the main aspects of *Gleichschaltung*:

- **Federal states:** the Nazis seized power in the federal states by 'legal' means. During the election campaign in February and March, the various federal states in Germany were 'brought into line'. Here, the position of the Nazi Frick as Reich

Minister of the Interior was important. The tactics were crude but successful. SA stormtroopers would create street disorders in provincial cities and towns. Frick was 'invited' to intervene by the local party bosses on the grounds that the existing authorities were incapable of keeping order. The local state governments were then forced to resign and were replaced by Nazi governments.

- **Trade unions:** the independent trade unions were abolished at the beginning of May and some of their leaders were taken to Dachau. They were replaced with one all-embracing 'union': the German Labour Front (DAF). This organisation theoretically represented the interests of workers of all classes ('workers of brain and brawn') and appeared to be compatible with the establishment of the 'folk community' (*Volksgemeinschaft*) (see page 30).

- **Civil service:** the Law for the Restoration of the Professional Civil Service, passed on 7 April 1933, forced the compulsory retirement of officials of non-Aryan descent. Jews were purged along with those who were known to be opponents of the Nazis. Many senior civil servants were in any case Nazi sympathisers.

- **Education system:** *Gleichschaltung* was pursued most fully in the education system. The many different youth organisations of the Weimar period were replaced by the Hitler Youth and the League of German Maidens, the only exception initially being those attached to the Catholic Church. Membership of the Hitler Youth was not made compulsory until March 1939. By the beginning of that year, approximately 1.75 million boys had joined.

The education system was purged of all its 'undesirable' teachers. In Prussia some 32% of head teachers in secondary schools had been dismissed by July 1934. The teachers' professional association, the National Socialist Teachers' League, became the sole union and by 1937, 97% of all teachers were members. The school curriculum was reorganised to comply with Nazi ideas on race and the *Volksgemeinschaft*.

Threats to Hitler's power

By the end of 1933 the regime claimed that all institutions had been coordinated. Whilst this is not strictly true, considerable progress in the Nazification of German society had been made by then. After 11 months of power, Hitler and the Nazis had eliminated all other parties, the trade unions and independent state governments throughout the German Reich. Hitler's position seemed secure. However, both the armed forces and the SA stormtroopers under Ernst Röhm could still pose a serious threat and their aims were mutually incompatible.

The growth in numbers and high-profile activity of the SA was increasingly a threat to Hitler's position as a respectable and responsible statesman. The conservative establishment was increasingly worried about the antics of the 'brown trash'. The leaders of the armed forces were concerned about Röhm's publicly proclaimed policies of merging the *Reichswehr* (the official Germany Army) with the SA. Hitler was worried about the growing insubordination of the SA rank and file, and by Röhm's claims that he and Hitler should hold joint power, with Röhm as the *Generalissimo* of the armed forces and Hitler merely the political figurehead.

There was a fundamental disagreement between Röhm and Hitler on the nature of the seizure of power that had occurred on 30 January 1933. For Röhm this was only the beginning. He disliked the fact that Hitler had to comply with the wishes of the traditional élites. Throughout 1933 he increasingly called for a 'second revolution' which would complete the Nazi national uprising by destroying the conservative forces that Hitler still relied on. Röhm's public posturing, the mass parades of armed SA forces and public demonstrations of SA power, combined with the thuggish activities of the rank and file on the streets, clearly damaged Hitler's claims of respectability at home and abroad.

By the spring of 1934 it was apparent that President Hindenburg did not have much longer to live. The old Field Marshal still had the loyalty and support of the Army leadership. Hitler's power could not be total until he could make himself the Führer of the German nation after the President's death and have all members of the armed forces swear a personal oath of allegiance to him. For this he would need the support of the Army commanders who demanded the right to be the sole bearers of arms in the Reich, and insisted on the destruction of the SA leadership.

Hitler was also hearing evidence from the SS leader Himmler and Gestapo chief Goering about a planned SA coup. As will be seen in the next area of focus (pages 16–19), there was great rivalry and hostility between Nazi leaders.

Hitler was indecisive. What appears to have jolted him into action was a speech made by von Papen at the University of Marburg on 17 June 1934. Here, the fears of the old élites were articulated. SA activities were condemned along with talk of a 'second revolution'. What was most serious for Hitler was the possibility that business, military and bureaucratic élites would combine to prevent him succeeding Hindenburg.

In the resulting Night of the Long Knives of 30 June 1934, Röhm and other SA leaders were arrested and subsequently murdered. The official number of those killed was put at 85 but some estimates put the figure as high as 200. Not all the victims were SA leaders. Hitler used the occasion to settle old scores. Gregor Strasser, who had been involved in Chancellor Kurt von Schleicher's attempt to split the NSDAP in December 1932, was shot, as was Schleicher himself. Papen was placed under house arrest, but the author of his Marburg speech, Edgar Jung, was shot. Essentially, in the 'Röhm Purge' (another name for the Night of the Long Knives) Hitler took the opportunity to kill those on both the left (SA) and the right (conservatives) who might possibly challenge him.

Hitler's decision to side with the *Reichswehr* in the Night of the Long Knives was of enormous significance for the following reasons:

- **Armed forces:** Hitler now had the support of the Army commanders and when Hindenburg died in August they willingly complied with the personal oath of allegiance sworn by all members of the armed forces on 20 August 1934. This was to be a major factor in explaining the failure of Army resistance plots.

- **SS state:** the purge, carried out by the SS, marked the rise of a sinister and infinitely more powerful organisation. Under the SS leader (*Reichsführer*) Heinrich Himmler, Nazi Germany was increasingly to become the SS state and the instrument of the Führer's will. (For more on the SS, see pages 19–22.)

- **Legal murder:** from the point of view of the rule of law, the actions Hitler took in the purge meant that whenever he felt there was a state of emergency, he alone could act for the German people. This was how he justified his actions to the Reichstag 2 weeks after the purge. In such emergencies there would be no need for trials and courts. Large-scale murder was thus legalised.

- **Public image:** a significant consequence of the purge was the use Goebbels, as Propaganda Minister, made of it. Hitler was presented in the press as having cleaned up the notoriously unpopular SA on behalf of the German people. Hitler's popularity rose to new heights.

Nazism: was Hitler 'master in the Third Reich' or 'weak dictator'?

This question has divided historians perhaps more than any other aspect of the Third Reich. For many years after 1945, the consensus among historians was that Hitler dominated the Nazi political system, that orders came down from above and were carried out with ruthless efficiency. The logic of this interpretation lies in the fact that Nazism rose and fell with Hitler, that Nazism was in fact 'Hitlerism', as pointed out by the German Karl Dietrich Bracher. According to this view, Hitler had a programme which in the main he held to from the 1920s until his death and his ideology became clear government policy. Nazi Germany was indeed a totalitarian state in practice as well as in theory.

From the mid-1960s, revisionist historians began to question the emphasis on the personal role of Hitler and the extent to which he was an absolute dictator. During the last two decades, a surprising picture of confusion and chaos in the Nazi political system has emerged. While this is now broadly accepted by historians, there is still disagreement about the reasons. For example, Karl Dietrich Bracher and Klaus Hildebrand have argued that this lack of coordination and confusion was deliberate. Hitler intended a policy of divide and rule so he could maintain his own position of supreme power. Such historians are known as *intentionalists*. In contrast, historians like Hans Mommsen and Martin Broszat argue that the confusions that existed reflected Hitler's limitations, his personal working style, the tendency for big 'empires' to develop within the Nazi system, his lack of interest in the day-to-day business of running a government and his general indecisiveness. These historians are called *structuralists* or *functionalists*. Mommsen summed up their position by describing Hitler as 'unwilling to take decisions, frequently uncertain, exclusively concerned with upholding his prestige and personal authority, influenced in the strongest fashion by his current entourage, in some respects a weak dictator'.

The key to an understanding of the workings of the Nazi political system lies in an appreciation of the differences between the theory and practice of Hitler's power. The constitutional theorist Ernst Rudolf Huber defined Hitler's power as follows:

> …we must not speak of 'state power' but of 'Führer power'. For it is not the state as an impersonal entity which is the source of political power but rather political power is given to the Führer as the executor of the nation's common will. Führer power is comprehensive and total: it unites within itself all means of creative political activity; it embraces all spheres of national life; it includes all comrades who are bound to the Führer in loyalty and obedience. Führer power is not restricted by safeguards and controls, by autonomous protected spheres, and by vested individual rights, but rather it is free and independent, exclusive and unlimited.

Hitler's power was thus defined in astonishingly vague, charismatic terms. Theoretically his power was total, unlimited and all-embracing. He had the right to exercise this power because he represented and executed the nation's will. This was clearly a vague and irrational reason for holding total power in a modern industrialised society of some 70 million. There was no constitution, no hereditary principle and no system for electing a leader. It was a highly personal form of power.

Führer power: theory and practice

Hitler showed little interest in the day-to-day business of running the government. He was bored by paperwork and was reluctant to put his signature to anything. As Führer, he was concerned with the great projects, the great visions; foreign, military and racial policies. He saw the bureaucratic detail associated with running the government as being beneath him.

Hitler had an extraordinarily bohemian, lazy lifestyle. He hated the capital, Berlin, seeing it as an architectural monstrosity plagued by communism. He would contrive to spend as much of his time as possible shut away in his mountain retreat at the Berghof in the Bavarian Alps. In the summer months he would often spend weeks at a time there, receiving foreign dignitaries. As part of his normal daily routine he would rise late, often after midday. He would spend a few minutes cursorily looking at official papers and government documents, often signing them without reading them. He would lunch, usually alone, scrutinising that day's press cuttings (his image, presented in the press, of course did interest him). He would then take a walk, usually alone, and on his return would settle down to watch Hollywood movies, often two in succession. In the evenings he would often invite guests for dinner. These tended to be old party comrades from the early Munich days rather than current Nazi leaders.

Hitler would conduct a rambling monologue, often lasting for hours on end, in which he would reminisce about the early days and pontificate. He would go to bed in the early hours and usually follow the same routine the next day.

There was no organised forum for the discussion of government policies. After 1934 the importance of the Reich Cabinet diminished and it did not meet at all after 1937. How, then, were government policy decisions made, and by whom? One of the most extraordinary documents that underpins the structuralist viewpoint is a statement made by Werner Willikens, State Secretary in the Ministry of Agriculture, in February 1934:

> Everyone who has the opportunity to observe it knows that the Führer can hardly dictate from above everything which he intends to realise sooner or later. On the contrary, up till now everyone with a post in the new Germany has worked best when he has, so to speak, worked towards the Führer…in fact it is the duty of everybody to try to work towards the Führer along the lines he would wish.

In reality, this is a comment on the vagueness and lack of clarity of leadership and orders from above. One had to use one's initiative and try to interpret or guess what the Führer's 'will' would be on any given subject. The problem consisted in knowing exactly what Hitler's 'will' was, given the rarity of Cabinet or other collective meetings, the fact that he shut himself away from Berlin for much of the time, that he was reluctant to commit himself to paper and that he was bored by routine governmental bureaucracy. The only solution was to have regular access to him. However, leading ministers in charge of government departments might go months or even years without seeing the Führer. As the postwar comments of Carl Schmitt, a constitutional lawyer, and Carl von Weizsacker, a Foreign Office official, stated: 'Ministerial skill consisted in making the most of a favourable hour or minute when Hitler made a decision, this often taking the form of a remark thrown out casually, which then went on its way as an "order of the Führer".'

According to the definition of 'Führer power', Hitler had a claim to be omnipotent (all-powerful) and omniscient (all-knowing). Clearly, given Hitler's lifestyle and leadership style, he could not be all-knowing. From the great quantities of mail that arrived daily, he would only be able to see what was pre-selected for him by his officials. He was reluctant to let himself be informed and this was complicated by the fact that he listened only to what he wanted to hear. The logical consequence of a situation like this is that eventually he was only told what his officials thought he wanted to hear.

In contrast to the traditional image of a firm and decisive leader, the picture that emerges is of a leader who was reluctant to make decisions. Hitler didn't want to intervene in disputes between leading party men, finding it difficult to work with large numbers of people. He hoped that things would sort themselves out on their own. It was a frustrating job for his secretaries, who tried to get decisions from him on important matters. Hitler would often make decisions on the spur of the moment without informing himself or being informed of the necessary detail. Often party leaders would attempt to get decisions from him over lunch or tea. It became very much a matter of catching the Führer at the right time.

In such a system of government, with a lack of clear orders or decisions from above, and with the necessity of interpreting the will of the Führer, it was almost inevitable that great 'empires' would develop. This was complicated by the fact that Hitler tended to create new ministries and departments — not to replace existing ones but to run parallel with them. The result was, as Hitler's press chief Otto Dietrich stated:

> In the 12 years of his rule in Germany Hitler produced the biggest confusion in government that has ever existed in a civilised state. During his period of government, he removed from the organisation of the state all clarity of leadership and produced a completely opaque network of competencies.

Essentially, Hitler created (or was unable to prevent the creation of, depending on whether an intentionalist or a structuralist viewpoint is taken) a confusing system of 'empires' in competition with each other and often with confusing, overlapping jurisdictions. To take one example, who was really in overall control of education policy, of such vital importance in the Nazi regime? Was it Bernhard Rust, the Education Minister; Joseph Goebbels, the Propaganda Minister; Heinrich Himmler, the head of the SS; Robert Ley, the leader of the DAF (German Labour Front); or was it Baldur von Schirach, the leader of the Hitler Youth? All of these 'empires' could claim to have an interest in the education of the young.

Given that one had to 'work towards the Führer's will' without clear guidelines or written orders, and given the overlapping of jurisdictions and responsibilities between 'empires' which were often in competition or conflict with each other, a process of what the historian Martin Broszat called 'cumulative radicalisation' tended to develop. Party leaders, faced with the task of pleasing or impressing Hitler, would tend to adopt the more radical of possible alternatives in the hope that in so doing they were implementing the Führer's will. One area for which this had ominous implications was the realm of Jewish policy.

The confusions and chaos described above suggest that the Nazi political system would sooner or later collapse because of its own internal contradictions. The argument put forward by a number of historians is that the whole system was held in check by the SS.

The role of the SS and the police state

The SS had its origins as Hitler's bodyguard in 1925. In the following 20 years it became the most feared and powerful 'empire' amongst the many which developed as a consequence of the Nazi political system. It became the party police of the Nazi movement, the 'aristocracy of National Socialism'. By the time of the Second World War it had a membership of around 1 million and had a controlling influence in the German war effort, with dominance in large areas of Nazi-controlled Europe. Conceived as the instrument of the Führer's will, the SS developed independently of the state and was not restrained by the legal system. By the eve of the war it had already assumed overall control of all policing in Germany, ultimate responsibility for the Jewish question, for ideology and propaganda, domestic security, and was gaining a foothold in the formation of foreign policy. It even owned more than 40 business enterprises. It developed a number of its own rituals, had its own form of wedding service and took a leading role in population and racial policies. All the leading Nazis were honorary members of the SS. It was distinct from the unruly brown-shirted SA and the Secret State Police Office (Gestapo).

From 1929 the SS was led by Heinrich Himmler in the role of *Reichsführer* SS. Himmler had joined the NSDAP as an agricultural student in 1921. He was a fanatical racist who believed utterly in the concept of the Aryan peoples as the 'master race' and for whom the life or death struggle between Aryans and Jews was the sole driving force of world history. Until the last few months of his life, Himmler remained totally loyal to Hitler. He shared with Hitler the *Lebensraum* theory — that Germany was a nation without space whose mission was to conquer and colonise whole areas of eastern Europe in order for the German peasant farmer to exploit the land and the racially inferior Slavs.

After becoming its leader, Himmler aimed to turn the SS into the élite institution of the Nazi movement. Having been raised in Catholic Bavaria, he based the organisation on the fanatical Catholic Jesuits. This meant total loyalty. All SS men had to dedicate themselves to the SS and swear an oath of loyalty to the Führer. SS men had to prove their credentials on racial and medical, rather than academic, grounds. Himmler saw the SS man as a political soldier, as distinct from the traditional military soldier. Whilst the conventional soldier fought against clearly defined external enemies in wartime, the political soldier had to fight against enemies, or potential enemies, everywhere, both abroad and particularly at home. In common with other totalitarian organisations, all of National Socialist Germany's enemies were reduced to one — in this case, the Jew. Thus, those who did not conform to the Nazi ideal of an Aryan 'folk community' (Marxists, freemasons, socialists, liberal opponents etc.) were all led ultimately by Jews. More specifically, domestic enemies of the SS were put into one of three categories: racial enemies who must be 'eradicated'; ideological enemies (Marxists, liberals, freemasons and socialists); or moral enemies — habitual criminals, homosexuals, social deviants, the mentally unfit — all generally classed as 'asocials'. These last two categories might be 're-educated' in concentration camps, although the 'asocials', deemed genetically inferior, would have to be sterilised.

Himmler and the SS

So all-embracing were the powers of the SS that many historians have defined Nazi Germany as the SS-police state. The main stages by which Himmler and the SS accumulated their power and influence are outlined below.

A special security service was established in 1931 with Reinhard Heydrich as its head. This was known as the SD. Heydrich was Himmler's deputy in the SS until his assassination in 1942.

On the appointment of Hitler as Chancellor in January 1933, the SS numbered not many more than 50,000 and was technically still subordinate to the much larger SA. Himmler, who saw the SA leader Ernst Röhm as a rival, wanted to eliminate the SA's influence and assume control of all policing as part of the struggle against domestic enemies. In April 1933 Himmler was promoted to 'Political Police Commander of Bavaria'. This was a prelude to his eventual assumption of a similar role for the entire Reich. By the beginning of 1934 Himmler was in control of the political police in all German states except Prussia.

The SS immediately gained influence over the concentration camp system, starting with Dachau in March 1933. It was supervised brutally by SS guards. Heydrich took the ultimate decision as to who was to be imprisoned and released. By 1937 there were three main concentration camps: Dachau, Buchenwald and Sachsenhausen.

In April 1933 Hermann Goering, the acting Prussian Minister of the Interior, formed the Prussian Secret State Police Office, known as the Gestapo. This was empowered to take into 'protective custody' all those suspected of being hostile to the Nazi regime. Increasingly fearful and suspicious of the activities of the SA leader, Röhm, Goering sought Himmler as an ally, and in April 1934 appointed him as Inspector of the Gestapo, although Himmler was still subordinate to Goering in the hierarchy.

It was the Night of the Long Knives, the purge of the SA leadership carried out by the SS, which confirmed Himmler's great rise in power and influence. The SS was now totally independent of the SA and Hitler gave support to Himmler in his bid to take control of the Gestapo, which he achieved by the beginning of 1935.

In 1936, in order to end the confusions caused by the overlapping functions of the Ministry of the Interior, Gestapo and SS, Hitler appointed Himmler as the chief of the German police. Most ominously, in that year the SS began to assume overall responsibility for Jewish policy.

By 1939 the SS had either total control or considerable influence in the following areas:

- **Ideology, culture and propaganda:** the SS sponsored many academic articles, books, films and scientific activities, all furthering the cause of the Aryan master race. The *Lebensborn* institutions, sponsored by the SS, enabled the procreation of racially pure children without regard for their legitimacy.
- **Domestic security:** after a few years the SS achieved complete control in all areas of maintenance of domestic security through the SD, police and control of the concentration camps. By 1939 the SS men chosen to guard the camps ('death's head units') numbered some 9,000.
- **SS units:** despite Hitler's promise to the Army leaders that after the Röhm purge the traditional armed forces would be the only bearers of weapons in Germany,

the SS leadership began to build a small army of its own, trained in military techniques. More than 14,000 men belonged to armed SS units by 1939.

- **Labour:** as the concentration camp system developed in the 1930s, the SS leadership increasingly saw the camps as large reservoirs of free or cheap labour. This was to be increased dramatically with the establishment of camps, mainly in Poland, in the early years of the war. By the end of the war, the SS owned a large number of factories involved in the production of a wide variety of goods.

The popularity of Hitler and the Nazis

This part of the guide focuses on the Nazis' use of propaganda, the creation of the 'Hitler myth', the extent of dissent and opposition to the regime and the reasons for the failure of resistance.

Basic assumptions of Nazi propaganda

In his book *Mein Kampf*, Hitler devoted much space to discussions of the aims, uses and assumptions of propaganda. The starting-point was that the common man in the modern industrialised society was more important than ever before. Through clever use of propaganda, Hitler and the Nazis were to articulate and exploit the fears and hopes of the mass of the population. The essential point was that propaganda should be kept simple. The aim was to find out what people's grievances were both locally and nationally and to offer scapegoats on which to heap the blame. In 1930, in an interview with Otto Strasser, a leading opponent within the Nazi Party, Hitler summed up the thinking behind the use of Nazi propaganda:

> The mass of the working classes want nothing but bread and games. They will never understand the meaning of an ideal, and we cannot hope to win them over to one. What we have to do is select from a new master-class men who will not allow themselves to be guided, like you, by the morality of pity. Those who rule must know they have the right to rule because they belong to a superior race.

This reflected Hitler's fundamental contempt for the masses. If you give them 'bread' (gainful employment, wages in their pocket) and provide them with 'games' (spectacular mass rallies; foreign policy successes; organised communal activities; the possibility of one day owning the new people's car, the Volkswagen) and if you make them feel they belong to a racially pure 'folk community' (*Volksgemeinschaft* — see page 30), then they will support you. Thus, to be effective, propaganda should:

- **be visual and oral** rather than written, hence the use of ritual mass rallies; great marches; the striking red, white and black colours of the swastika flag; the use of uniforms with the brown-shirted SA creating an impression of youth and virility;
- **appeal to the basic gut emotions and instincts** of the people rather than to reason. The message should be simplified: the emphasis on youth as the master race of tomorrow; contempt for communists, socialists, Jews, liberals, all those who don't conform to the idea of the 'folk community'; the evils of the Versailles peace treaty and the Weimar system that signed it, and so on.

The *medium* was seen as being as important as the message. Hitler, in the early days, often referred to himself as the 'drummer of the masses' (*der Trommler*). Much has been written about Hitler's extraordinary abilities as a public speaker. He could regularly hold people's attention for up to 3 hours, often making the same basic points again and again. It was not what Hitler said but the way he said it. He was a master at gauging the atmosphere of an audience. Often he would wait for a whole minute in front of a mass audience, assessing the mood before beginning quietly, sometimes haltingly and hesitantly. Before long he would be into his stride, ranting, raving, alternately hooking his thumb round his belt, brushing back his hair, standing on the balls of his feet when making a decisive point. Sometimes he would adopt a simple question-and-answer routine in engaging with the audience. The climax would come and the speech would end with thousands of *Heil Hitlers*. Even if some were doubtful about the things Hitler had said, they were swept along by the great outburst of acclaim for the Führer.

The role of Joseph Goebbels

There had to be more to it than the stage management of mass rallies, giant propaganda showpieces and Hitler's oratory. The man credited with the creation of the Hitler myth was Joseph Goebbels, appointed the Reich Minister for Propaganda and Enlightenment in March 1933. The essence of the Hitler myth was that the Führer was simultaneously a man of the people and one who stood above the people. In contrast to Hindenburg, the Prussian aristocrat and Army commander blessed with the privileges of high birth and social status, Hitler was the decorated front-line soldier of the First World War, a man who understood and had shared the fears, sufferings and anxieties of the common man. Hitler was the plain man who spoke directly to the people not as a politician but as the leader of a movement. However, the Führer was more than a mere common man. By his extraordinary willpower — his 'will to power' — he had risen above the common herd to achieve the status of a 'superman'.

Hitler was presented as being above the party. Indeed, Goebbels deliberately aimed to separate the Führer from the party. Hitler was the father figure, the *Ersatzkaiser* who had been lacking in Germany since the abdication of William II in 1918. He was the saviour who had deliberately forsaken marriage and having children in order to save and serve the fatherland. Indeed, Hitler was blessed with mystical, almost religious qualities.

Goebbels had said that 'power rests on the will of the masses'. In true totalitarian fashion he saw his task as being the need to channel the collective will towards the objectives of the regime, to mobilise opinion. The official task of Goebbels' new ministry was stated as 'the spreading of enlightenment and propaganda within the population concerning the policy of the Reich government and the national reconstruction of the German fatherland'. The main media for indoctrination were radio, the press, film, theatre and the arts.

Much emphasis was placed on the use of radio and by April 1934, Goebbels had effectively 'coordinated' the radio network into his ministry. Radios were made cheap to buy and by 1939 some 70% of German homes had one. 'Community listening' was encouraged in offices, factories and cafés. Loudspeakers were installed at strategic points in the streets of towns.

By February 1934 Goebbels' ministry had effective control of all newspaper publication. At the daily press conferences, editors were given directives from the Propaganda Ministry on the presentation and treatment of news.

Goebbels had a great interest in the cinema. It was a form of leisure that was rapidly increasing in popularity in the 1930s. The regime exerted less direct control over the cinema than it did over radio and the press. Indeed, more than 1,000 films were made between 1933 and 1945, and only a minority of them were used directly for propaganda purposes. The most famous propaganda film was Leni Riefenstahl's *Triumph of the Will* (1935), about the Nuremberg rally of 1934. The most notorious was the anti-Semitic *The Eternal Jew*. During the later stages of the war in 1944, when there was an increasing need to boost the morale of the civilian population, Goebbels transferred around 100,000 much-needed soldiers from the front in order to make a film about the heroic German resistance to Napoleon. In general, though, the cinema was regarded by the regime as a diversion for the public, a form of entertainment, the 'games' in Hitler's 'bread and games'.

In the arts generally, the Nazis attempted to create a people's culture. Nazi art was to be anti-modernist and 'German'. Art was to be seen as an expression of race. It was to glorify the strong and the heroic. The works of Jewish, liberal and socialist artists and writers were purged, and on 10 May 1933 the infamous burning of books took place.

An obvious aim of Nazi propaganda was to get people to conform. To this end '*Heil Hitler*' became the official form of greeting. In order to rival the festivals in the religious calendar, important dates in the Nazi year were celebrated: the anniversary of Hitler's appointment as Chancellor, Hitler's birthday, a commemoration of those who died in the Munich Putsch of 1923 and so on.

Hitler's personal popularity

At least until 1944, Hitler's personal popularity was considerable. The historian Ian Kershaw has pointed out that whereas only one-third of the German population voted for the Nazi Party or actually supported it, about nine-tenths supported Hitler. Partly this was as a consequence of Goebbels' propaganda. While there was increasing disgust and resentment of the 'little Hitlers' — the local, corrupt and often brutal party bosses — Hitler was usually exempt from blame. 'If only the Führer knew' was a common statement.

There were probably three distinct periods in which Hitler's popularity was at a peak. After the Night of the Long Knives, Hitler was seen as having dealt with the increasingly frightening and unpopular SA. His popularity rose with each foreign policy success in the late 1930s, when Germany had repeatedly snubbed foreign opinion and destroyed the hated Versailles settlement without causing the loss of a single German life. During the peacetime years, Hitler's popularity rose to unprecedented levels just after the signing of the Munich Agreement with Chamberlain in the autumn of 1938. Goebbels portrayed Hitler as having saved Germany — and Europe — from war. During the first 2 years of the war, when Hitler was seen to be a more successful military commander than Alexander the Great or Napoleon, he had been repeatedly proved right and his doubting generals wrong. This is an important element in considering why most of Hitler's senior Army officers continued to support him until at least 1944, when the war was clearly being lost.

Dissent, opposition and resistance in the Third Reich

It is important to differentiate between these three words. Dissent implies grumbling, disagreement with aspects of the regime, possibly disillusionment, but little more. Opposition implies a public stance, a voicing of criticism either individually or as a body. Resistance implies an active attempt to overthrow Hitler and/or the regime. There were elements of all three during the 12 years of the Third Reich. Ian Kershaw's study of opinion in Bavaria has revealed that amongst peasants, workers and the lower-middle class generally, there were increasing complaints about consumer goods shortages, decline in real wages, food prices and so on. Such complaints were, however, essentially about economic and material factors. Where there were some elements of opposition and resistance was in the churches and the Army.

It is also important to bear in mind the difficulty of finding accurate and objective source material on the question of public opinion, opposition and resistance in a police state like Nazi Germany. The two main types of source material — reports by the regime itself, from the Gestapo and the SD, and reports written by SPD-contact men in Germany, prepared for socialist leaders in exile — are both imperfect. Opinion in a state with totalitarian ambitions is likely to be manufactured. Given that it was difficult to speak openly and honestly about the regime in public, it is difficult for historians to assess accurately the extent of opposition to the regime.

Opposition by the churches

Both the Protestant and Catholic Churches shared some of the ideals of Nazism: social and political conservatism, anti-communism and, to a certain extent, anti-Semitism. Opposition from the Protestants was caused by the regime's attempt to 'Nazify' the Church with the German Christian movement. In response to attempts to remove the Old Testament from the Bible, Pastor Martin Niemoller led the Pastors' Emergency League. The regime responded by arresting some Lutheran bishops, provoking a mass demonstration by orthodox Protestants in Nuremberg in September 1934. This led to a formal split, with the Pastors' Emergency League forming its own 'confessional' church. Martin Niemoller eventually served 8 years in various concentration camps, although he did survive the war.

More serious opposition came from the Catholic Church. The terms of the concordat of 1933 between the regime and the papacy stipulated that Catholic worship and influence over education would not be tampered with. By 1934 it was apparent that this was not the case. Theology was being relegated in importance as a school subject and the regime was attempting to remove crucifixes from Catholic schools. In December 1936, Bavarian bishops voiced their dissent and such was the traditional strength of Catholicism, especially in Bavaria, that the crucifixes had to be replaced.

It was the regime's euthanasia campaign that provoked the most serious opposition from the Church. In December 1940 the Vatican condemned euthanasia as being against the law of God. On 3 August 1941 the Bishop of Münster, Cardinal Galen, preached a sermon condemning the practice. Printed copies of the sermon were circulated. So strong was the outcry that Hitler ordered a halt to the campaign, although it did continue in a different form.

Clearly, there was dissent and opposition from both churches, but it is important to bear in mind that in both cases opposition was provoked only when the direct interests of the churches were affected. In neither case did the churches seem to stand back and survey the unsavoury aspects — the beatings up and killings of Jews and communists, the restrictions on civil liberties — still less condemn them publicly.

Opposition and resistance by the armed forces

Serious, organised resistance from sections of the Army High Command began in 1938. This was inspired by increasing fears about the aggressive nature of Hitler's foreign policy and the growing possibility of a war with Britain, France or Russia. There was a coup planned for the autumn of 1938, attempting to pre-empt Hitler's planned invasion of Czechoslovakia. Hitler was to be replaced by a constitutional monarchy, with a grandson of Kaiser William II becoming King. However, the plotters were divided on how to deal with Hitler. Some wanted Hitler to be put on trial while others wanted to have him declared insane by medical authorities. It was hoped that support would be gained from Britain and France.

The plot was being hatched at the time of the Czech crisis in September 1938. It was hoped and assumed that both Chamberlain and Hitler would stand firm, and with the real prospect of war the plotters would have justification in arresting Hitler. The plot was foiled by Chamberlain giving way and signing the Munich Agreement. Hitler, having deliberately created a war scare, was now seen in Germany as the great saviour of peace. So great was Hitler's popularity that the plotters were forced to abandon the attempt. After Munich, between 1939 and 1941, the chances of a successful plot receded dramatically as Hitler's foreign policy and military successes mounted. It was not until 1943, when the tide of war was clearly turning against Germany on the Eastern Front, that attempts to kill or depose Hitler resumed in a serious fashion — although isolated, usually badly conceived, attempts were made before then.

The most famous of the attempts on Hitler's life was the bomb plot of 20 July 1944. Hitler was to address a meeting at the 'Wolf's Lair' at Rastenburg in East Prussia. Colonel von Stauffenberg, the leader of the plot, was to plant a bomb in a briefcase in the thick concrete-walled building in which the meeting was to be held. At the last minute the meeting was moved to a wooden-walled hut, which would minimise the blast from the explosion. The briefcase containing the bomb was accidentally pushed under a heavy tabletop near to where Hitler was speaking. When the explosion occurred Hitler was slightly wounded and shaken, but nothing more. Thereafter there was a widespread and savage repression of all those suspected of conspiracy and there were no more serious, organised attempts on Hitler's life.

If any institution was capable of deposing or killing Hitler it was the Army, so why did it make so few real attempts and why did any attempts have little chance of succeeding? The main reasons are as follows:

- **Oath of personal allegiance to Hitler:** all members of the armed forces had to swear this oath after the death of Hindenburg. Hitler was now Head of State and Führer of the German nation. To attempt to depose him would be seen as an act of treason. Moreover, for the German officer particularly, it was a matter of honour to uphold the oath, whatever reservations he might hold.

- **Nazi indoctrination:** by the late 1930s, many junior officers had been thoroughly indoctrinated in Nazi ideology. Clearly, the removal of Hitler alone would be insufficient. Any plotters would have to consider how far down the regime's hierarchy they should go. The SS would be a formidable obstacle. In addition to this, in keeping with Hitler's style of leadership, a network of authorities with overlapping jurisdictions had been created. There was the OKW (High Command of the Armed Forces), separate high commands for the Army and Navy, and the RSHA (the central Reich security office), in which Himmler supervised the SD, Gestapo and all police.

- **Lack of help from the Allies:** help from the Allies was vital for the attempt to succeed. However, in 1938 the plotters were essentially foiled by the British and French policies of appeasement. During the later stages of the war, the Allies adopted a policy of unconditional surrender, which precluded the possibility of lending large-scale support to the subversion of the regime from within.

- **Access to Hitler:** particularly during the war, Hitler himself made it very difficult for would-be assassins. For reasons of security he avoided fixed schedules and often changed his plans at the last moment. After 1943 he travelled much less frequently. It was difficult to know his exact whereabouts in advance and gain access to him.

- **Defence of Germany:** Army officers really only considered overthrowing Hitler when they thought his foreign and military policies were too dangerous. The ground was cut from their feet with the extraordinary German military successes in the first 2 years of war. It was only when the war turned against Germany that serious attempts resumed, but by this time Germany was fighting a life-or-death struggle against the Red Army. German Army officers faced a dilemma — should they overthrow Hitler but in the process render Germany vulnerable to total occupation by the Russians, or should they put the emphasis on defending Germany at all costs against the hated and feared Bolsheviks? The overwhelming majority chose the latter.

Opposition and dissent by German youth

Not all young Germans were attracted to the Hitler Youth organisation or the League of German Maidens. Some resented the stifling regimentation and new groups sprang up as a direct protest against Nazism. They went by various umbrella names such as 'Swing Youth' or 'Edelweiss Pirates'. They had no coherent programme and often their protests were limited to specific forms of dress. During the war they focused on beating up members of the Hitler Youth, putting up anti-Nazi posters, listening to BBC broadcasts and helping German deserters. Many were imprisoned and some were executed.

The most famous form of protest came from the Munich 'White Rose' group. Hans and Sophie Scholl attended Munich University and by 1942 were distributing leaflets demanding the restoration of personal and political freedom. When news of the impending defeat at Stalingrad reached them they organised a demonstration of students against the Nazis in January 1943. They were arrested and executed and the group was broken up.

Why was opposition so ineffective?

There were many reasons why opposition to the Nazi regime was weak:

- It was difficult to appeal to people when the regime regularly organised plebiscites — which were often rigged. The regular and overwhelming 'yes' votes created an impression of great popularity of the regime, especially after the provision of full employment and foreign policy successes.

- Linked with this was Hitler's great and consistent popularity. Since Hitler was the embodiment of the Nazi regime, opposition was difficult to organise.

- Active opposition was difficult to organise when the regime controlled all aspects of the media.
- There was no effective institution that could successfully challenge the regime. Under the Nazis, society was atomised and depoliticised. The socialists and communists on the left were totally isolated and persecuted. The churches were more concerned to protect their own interests, and the personal oath of loyalty to Hitler effectively tied the armed forces to the regime.
- Sheer terror and the creation of the police state meant that dissent and opposition were very risky. The terrible punishments were a deterrent and the Gestapo had an effective police-spy network.
- Despite the fact that the majority of German people had not wanted war, during the years 1939–41 Nazi military successes were so striking, with comparatively little loss of German life, that it was very difficult for opponents in the totalitarian conditions of 'total war' to organise support for their cause. Such people would be seen as traitors in wartime. Similarly, when the war turned against the Germans and as German casualties grew on the Russian Front, most families had a male member risking his life at the front. Moreover, in the later stages of the war, with the Allies' mass bombing raids on German cities, German civilians had a dual focal point for hatred and it was not Hitler and the Nazis, but the Russians and the RAF.
- Perhaps the fundamental reason is the one most difficult to come to terms with: basic selfishness and sheer indifference to moral rights and wrongs and the sufferings of others. 'Bread and games' had been provided for the majority. Most people could experience some benefits from the regime, shutting themselves off from many of its basic cruelties and focusing entirely on what the regime had provided for them. In his study of opinion in Bavaria, Ian Kershaw noted that there was a tendency to 'retreat into the private sphere'. In peacetime, what fundamentally concerned the majority were material conditions: food prices, wages, general cost of living and so on. There were instances of peasants and workers showing dissent, but it never went further than that. It never became political. During the war, what concerned most people was the fate of loved ones at the front, not the wider moral issues of what was right or wrong with the Nazi system.

The persecution of the Jews

The focus in this part of the option is on the implementation of Nazi anti-Semitic policies, culminating in the Holocaust.

The *Volksgemeinschaft*

Central to Nazi ideology was the notion of a 'folk community' (*Volksgemeinschaft*). This was the establishment of a classless society of racially pure Germans. It would involve the mobilisation of the German people in the interests of greater national awareness. The German nation was supreme, and regional, religious and class loyalties were to be abandoned in the pursuit of the ideal of the nation. Young people were to be educated and trained to be racially aware and physically fit. Women were to be educated in their fundamental and vital role as mothers of Aryan children. The German Labour Front (DAF) replaced the old working-class trade unions and claimed to represent all German workers, whatever their status. Everybody in the nation was theoretically equal before the Führer.

These were very ambitious social aims and they would require the transformation of social and mental attitudes on a grand scale. The extent to which the *Volksgemeinschaft* was actually achieved is difficult to assess. Evidence from Kershaw's study of Bavaria suggests that it had a very limited impact, and that it was more of a propaganda myth than a reality.

It was the implications of the *Volksgemeinschaft* which were particularly ominous. Not only did it require total conformity, it also required the marginalisation and subsequent persecution of all those who didn't conform or belong. This included the mentally ill or physically deformed, even if they were of Aryan stock, political opponents like socialists, communists and liberals, habitual criminals, 'social deviants', homosexuals, supporters of obscure religious cults and all those who did not belong to the superior race.

Anti-Semitism in Nazi ideology

One aspect of the *Volksgemeinschaft* where the Nazis could claim to have achieved success was in their anti-Semitic policies. Racism, in particular anti-Semitism, was at the core of Nazi ideology. Point 4 of the 25-point programme of 1920 stated clearly that 'no Jew may be a member of the nation'. Hitler's *Mein Kampf* was full of references to the 'Jew'. The 'Jew' was seen to be poisoning Aryan culture and civilisation, through manipulation of international finance on the one hand and manipulation and control of the Russian Bolshevik Party on the other; hence the constant references to the 'Jew–Bolshevik conspiracy'. Senior Nazis were fond of referring to the Jew as a carrier of plague and disease. Jews were likened to rats. The Nazi mission therefore was to engage in a life or death struggle to combat the 'evils' of international Jewry.

Whether Hitler and the Nazis intended a physical destruction of the Jewish race from the beginning has been a question much disputed by leading historians. The intentionalists point to *Mein Kampf* and in particular to a notorious passage where

Hitler wishes for the gassing of thousands of Jews as punishment for causing the sacrifice of millions of German soldiers in the trenches. They also emphasise the fact that as the Nazi regime became more secure in the 1930s and grew in confidence in foreign policies, so the measures taken against the Jews became progressively more vicious and radical. A key aspect of the intentionalist argument is reference to Hitler's speech in the Reichstag on 30 January 1939, the sixth anniversary of his appointment as Chancellor. Here, referring to the increasing fears of a general European war, Hitler said that if war did come, it would have been caused by the Jews, and would result in their annihilation. The fact that the systematic destruction of the Jews in specially designed death camps occurred *after* the Nazi invasion of Soviet Russia in the summer of 1941 is seen as further proof that the eventual Final Solution, or Holocaust, was the culmination of a policy that had been intended as early as the 1920s.

An alternative view, the structuralist/functionalist argument, places far less emphasis on the notion of an *intended* policy of destruction, and far more emphasis on the immediate circumstances of the war in eastern Europe, particularly after 1941. Because of their extraordinary military successes in the first 2 years of war, the Nazis found themselves in control of millions of 'subhuman' Jews in Poland and western Russia. Having failed with various emigration policies such as settling European Jews on the island of Madagascar, or between the rivers Vistula and Bug in Poland, by the late autumn of 1941 the Nazi hierarchy was considering the idea of settling the Jews east of the Ural mountains in Siberia. This, of course, depended on the rapid defeat of Soviet Russia, which for a brief time looked possible. However, time was increasingly important. The hundreds of thousands of Jews herded into filthy ghettos, who had to be guarded and only a few of whom could be used for labour in the war effort, were now causing a problem due to lack of hygiene and a consequent spread of disease. Moreover, the Red Army, having retreated hundreds of miles in the first weeks and months of the Nazi–Soviet war, was now beginning to consolidate its positions and was showing signs of holding out for longer than had originally been expected. It was this set of circumstances which, according to the functionalist school, led to the establishment of the gas chambers.

The genesis of the Holocaust

It is not clear exactly when, and by whom, the decision to launch a Final Solution or systematic destruction of the Jews was taken. All that is known is that at some time between the invasion of Russia in the summer of 1941 and January 1942 the liquidation of the Jews moved from the comparatively haphazard approach of the first 2 years of war (during which time hundreds of thousands of Jews had already been slaughtered by gas vans, large-scale firing squads etc.) to the policy of deliberate genocide on a mass, 'industrialised' scale. Most historians now accept that it was a meeting in the Berlin suburb of the Wannsee on 20 January 1942 that set in motion the practical arrangements for the building of an extension to Auschwitz-Birkenau, the labour camp in Poland. 'Auschwitz II', and subsequently 'Auschwitz III', are the names most readily associated with the Holocaust.

Whether one accepts the intentionalist or functionalist interpretation of events, the following factors should be taken into account when considering the genesis of the Holocaust:

- **Written source material:** clear written evidence is hard to come by or to interpret with any exactitude. Partly this is because the SS-Nazi hierarchy tended to write and talk in euphemisms. There are references to the 'destruction' of the Jews and the words 'Final Solution' figure in correspondence between Nazi leaders. There is talk of 'dealing with the Jewish problem once and for all'. As with Hitler's annihilation speech of January 1939, historians are left to interpret these expressions as they will.

- **Authorisation of the Final Solution:** no signed, written order from Hitler authorising the Final Solution has been found. Although it is possible that such an order might have existed and was subsequently destroyed because of its sensitive nature, this is unlikely. It was not Hitler's style to commit himself in writing to anything unless absolutely necessary and naturally he would not want his name associated with a direct policy of mass genocide. It is quite likely that at some time during the crucial summer/autumn months of 1941 Hitler, in conversation with SS leaders like Himmler, Heydrich or Adolf Eichmann, expressed a desire that the 'Jewish business' finally be settled now that Germany was at war with 'Jew–Bolshevik' Russia. This was construed as 'an order of the Führer'. In other words, in keeping with his style, Hitler verbally authorised the wholescale destruction of the Jews but was not much concerned with exactly how this was to be achieved. It is at this point that Broszat's notion of 'cumulative radicalisation' (see page 19) came into play.

- **Military link:** although a distinction has been made between the 'unsystematic' mass slaughter of Jews and the 'systematic' use of gas chambers from 1942 onwards, this is somewhat artificial. The principle of slaughtering Jews was put into practice right at the beginning of the invasion of Poland in 1939, as the specially composed SS *Einsatzgruppen* units followed the German Army into Warsaw and carried out large-scale acts of murder. This was stepped up considerably in the summer of 1941 when the whole of western Russia was overrun by the Nazis. A major aspect of the intentionalist argument is the fact that as soon as the war started, under the secrecy and brutalised conditions of 'total war' on the Eastern Front, the need for military conquest was linked with the aim of physically destroying the Jews.

The main stages of persecution, 1933–39

On coming to power neither Hitler nor the Nazi hierarchy as a whole had a structured or coherent programme for dealing with the Jews in Germany. As has been seen, Hitler had to be seen to be respectable at home and abroad during the first years of power. Well-publicised and vicious attacks against the Jews might well have alienated the very forces of conservative society on which Hitler initially relied (hence Hitler's increasing concern about the activities of the SA during 1933–34). At this stage, persecution of the Jews had a far lower priority than the need to restore employment and the consolidation of power. Moreover, a significant proportion of Germany's half million Jewish population occupied important positions in business. There was therefore a piecemeal and rather unsystematic approach to the 'Jewish question' between 1933 and 1936, at least. It can be argued, though, that with the SS taking full responsibility for Jewish policy after 1936, anti-Semitic measures became more systematic and certainly more radical and extreme. In the 1930s, what began with comparatively 'mild' removal of Jews from the professions led to the notorious Nuremberg Laws of 1935 and culminated with the first large-scale and vicious pogrom of Jews in Kristallnacht in 1938. The following is a brief outline of the way in which measures against the Jews progressed:

- **1933** Beginning with a failed boycott of Jewish businesses, the Nazi government attempted to 'legalise' the persecution of the Jews by a series of measures restricting Jews from the civil service, limiting their ability to practise as doctors and dentists, excluding them from the journalistic profession and limiting the numbers of Jewish children attending German schools.

- **1935** This policy of piecemeal 'legal' persecution helped to fit Hitler's 'respectable' image, but did not satisfy the rank-and-file party activists who wanted a far more radical approach. This culminated in the Nuremberg Laws of September 1935 where Hitler was pressurised into announcing a major new policy initiative at the Nuremberg rally. The 'Law For The Protection of German Blood and Honour' and the 'Reich Citizenship Law' forbade physical relations between Jews and Aryans and formally and 'legally' prevented Jews from being citizens of the nation. Thus began the formal process of marginalising and isolating the Jews in Germany.

- **1936** Because Berlin was hosting the Olympic Games of 1936, Hitler ordered the toning down of attacks against the Jews because of the large number of foreign correspondents in Germany. But then a sinister development took place with the SS's assumption of large areas of 'Jewish policy'. Adolf Eichmann began a policy of actively encouraging German Jews to emigrate. However, it was financially and practically very difficult for Jewish families to uproot themselves and travel to western Europe or the USA. Many German Jews tried to seek refuge in the assumption that the Nazi regime was only a temporary nightmare. Moreover, during the late 1930s the USA and western Europe were still recovering from the Depression and would not welcome large numbers of Jews swelling the ranks of the unemployed. It is estimated that by 1939 about half of Germany's half million Jews had emigrated.

- **1937–38** Another ominous sign was the general radicalisation of Nazi policies, both in the domestic and foreign policy spheres. By 1937, Germany's economic position was much stronger. Conservative-minded government ministers and generals were dismissed and replaced with Nazi hardliners. With the Anschluss, the German takeover of Austria in March 1938, many more Jews and Jewish businesses came into Nazi hands.

- **1938** In the wake of the Anschluss, more steps were taken to legalise the Nazi strategies against the Jews, many of them complementing, or taking to radical extremes, the measures of 1933. For example, on 17 July a decree was issued facilitating the identification of Jews.

    On 9 November, the anniversary of the failed Munich Putsch of 1923, Kristallnacht — by far the most violent attack on the Jews to date — occurred. The name, translating as 'Crystal Night', refers to the shattered glass on the streets of major German cities after a night of unprecedented violence against Jews, particularly shopkeepers. Officially, 91 Jews were killed but the real number was probably far higher.

    This can be seen as a useful example of 'cumulative radicalisation' and 'working towards the Führer's will'. Goebbels had fallen out of favour with Hitler because of the embarrassment caused by his affair with a Czech actress. To win his way back to favour, Goebbels seized on the murder of a minor official in the German Embassy in Paris as a pretext for the launching of a nationwide pogrom of Jewish property on the anniversary of the Munich Putsch, which could be portrayed as a spontaneous eruption of violent anti-Semitic feelings by the German nation. In reality, much of the violence was organised and directed by the remnants of the SA, dressed in civilian clothes. Goebbels intended to please Hitler with a propaganda coup which would similarly satisfy the Führer's claim simply to be carrying out the wishes of the German people and the radical party rank and file by 'giving the SA their last fling'.

- **1939** By the eve of the war in 1939, the situation of the Jews in Germany had become progressively worse. They were now isolated and marginalised in German society by vicious anti-Semitic propaganda in schools, the cinema and the press. They had been removed from all professional positions in society. They were forbidden to mix in any way with Aryans and from November 1938 they were forced to wear the yellow Star of David badge. Moreover, their fate was increasingly in the hands of the violent, ruthless, fanatically racist leaders of the SS — men like Himmler, Heydrich and Eichmann.

Questions
&
Answers

AS History

In this section there are four specimen exam questions, each on a different theme within the option:

(1) The consolidation of Hitler's power, 1933–34.
(2) The Nazi system of government.
(3) The popularity of Hitler and opposition to him.
(4) Nazi anti-Semitic policies, 1933–39.

The four topics chosen are clearly defined areas within the specification. However, the examiners might select four passages from different topic areas with a common fundamental theme. Therefore, in preparation for the exam, you should not compartmentalise your revision and simply revise some topics and not others.

Resist the temptation to study the answers before you have attempted the questions. In the exam you will be asked to answer one three-part structured question in 1 hour. Practise doing each answer under timed exam conditions, then compare your answers with the worked responses supplied.

In each of the four worked responses the marks awarded would be in the A-grade category. In addition, there is one example of a C-grade response. The examiners' mark schemes for each question should help you to see exactly what examiners are looking for in order to award high marks.

In all four of the A-grade examples, the answers put the relevant passages into their historical context. This means using your own knowledge of the topic in conjunction with the information in the given passage(s). Examiner comments (preceded by the icon *e*) are given for each of the answers, but the following features are common to all A-grade responses:

- Good use of outside knowledge is made to put the passages into context.
- The sources are evaluated where necessary and the information in the passages is interpreted in the light of the question.
- The answers focus on the question without drifting off into irrelevant or semi-relevant padding. This is particularly important on the mini-essay in question (c), which carries 60 marks.

The consolidation of Hitler's power

(a) **Study Source A**
From this source and your own knowledge, explain the reference to 'communist acts of violence'. (20 marks)

(b) **Study Sources B and C**
Compare Hitler's and Röhm's aims in 1933 and explain the differences. (40 marks)

(c) **Using all the sources**
From your own knowledge and these sources, discuss the view that Hitler consolidated his power between 1933 and 1934 by 'semi-legal' means. (60 marks)

Source A: *Decree of the Reich President for the Protection of People and State, 28 February 1933*

By the authority of section 48 of the German constitution the following is decreed as a defensive measure against communist acts of violence endangering the state:

The restrictions on personal liberty, on the right of free expression of opinion, including freedom of the press, on the right of assembly and association, and violations of the privacy of postal, telegraphic and telephone communications, and warrants for house searches, orders for confiscations as well as restrictions on property rights are permissible beyond the legal limits otherwise prescribed.

Source B: *Minutes of a cabinet meeting, 7 March 1933*

The Reich Chancellor opened the meeting and stated that...he regarded the events of 5 March as a revolution. Ultimately Marxism would no longer exist in Germany.

What was needed was an Enabling Law passed by a two-thirds majority. He, the Reich Chancellor, was firmly convinced that the Reichstag would pass such a law. The deputies of the German Communist Party would not appear at the opening of the Reichstag because they were in jail....

The Vice-Chancellor and Reich Commissioner of Prussia (Papen) expressed to the Reich Chancellor and the National Socialist Organisation the thanks of the Reich Cabinet for their admirable performance in the election....

With regard to the internal political situation, the Vice-Chancellor stated that yesterday (6 March) Dr Kaas had been to see him. He had stated that he had come without previously consulting his party and was now prepared to let bygones be bygones. He had moreover offered the cooperation of the Centre Party.

question 1

AS History

Source C: *SA leader Ernst Röhm writes a newspaper article published in June 1933*

The course of events between 30 January and 21 March 1933 does not represent the sense and meaning of the German National Socialist revolution....

The SA and SS will not tolerate the German revolution going to sleep or being betrayed at the half-way stage by non-combatants. Not for their own sake, but for Germany's sake. For the brown army is the last levy of the nation, the last bastion against communism....

It is in fact high time the national revolution stopped and became the National Socialist one. Whether they like it or not, we will continue our struggle...*with* them; if they are unwilling — *without* them; and if necessary *against* them!

Source D: *Minutes of the cabinet meeting of 3 July 1934 after the Röhm purge*

The Reich Chancellor...began by giving a detailed account of the origin and suppression of the high treason plot. The Reich Chancellor stressed that lightning action had been necessary, otherwise many thousands of people would have been in danger of being wiped out.

Defence Minister General von Blomberg thanked the Führer in the name of the Reich cabinet and the army for his determined and courageous action, by which he had saved the German people from civil war. The Führer had shown greatness as a statesman and soldier....

The Reich Cabinet then approved a law on measures for the self-defence of the state. Its single paragraph reads:

'The measures taken on 30 June and 1 and 2 July to suppress acts of high treason are legal, being necessary for the self-defence of the state.'

Reich Minister of Justice Dr Gurtner commented that measures of self-defence taken before the imminent occurrence of a treasonable action should be considered not only legal but the duty of a statesman.

■ ■ ■

Mark scheme

(a) Comprehension of a source
To gain a mark in the higher band, the reference must be understood in its historical context. For band A you must demonstrate a clear understanding of the reasons why the communists were seen as a threat. Knowledge of the message of the 'national uprising' and the election campaign is required at this level. Better answers might not just refer to the Reichstag fire, but to the significance of the decree that followed.

Lower-level answers would only refer to the fire and the decree without really putting both into the context of the election campaign and Hitler's objectives.

(b) Comparison of two sources
For marks in band A, consideration would have to be given to Hitler's need to stabilise his position at home and abroad; his public image and the bad image publicly of the 'brown trash'; and Hitler's need to reassure the traditional élites in the business world, civil service and especially the Army that he was 'safe' and proceeding 'legally'. In addition, the higher marks would go to those who drew on their knowledge of the fundamental tensions existing between the SA leadership and Hitler from the moment he was appointed Chancellor. Good linking between the sources and wider knowledge would be necessary for the highest marks. Röhm's aims for a 'second' revolution would have to be compared with Hitler's need to be 'legal' as shown in Source B.

(c) Judgement in context, based on a set of sources and own knowledge
Effective linking of wider knowledge and the information given in the passages would be needed for marks in band A. All the sources would have to be put into the context of the consolidation of Hitler's power, 1933–34.

Source A provides the 'legal' basis for acting arbitrarily and dictatorially in a state of emergency, this decree being authorised by the Reich President.

Source B refers to the 'constitutionally correct' desire to secure the two-thirds majority for what was to be an effective emasculation of the independence of the Reichstag. The communists would not be there to vote against the Enabling Law because they had 'legally' been outlawed by the Fire Decree etc.

Source C reveals the difference between Röhm's 'illegal' desires and Hitler's 'legal' and 'constitutional' ones, with Röhm setting himself up as a potential threat to the security of the state.

Source D (the justification of the purge) could be given with reference to the 'state of emergency' implied by the Reichstag Fire Decree. Hindenburg was still President, so Hitler was only acting 'legally' in defending the President's authority and the security of the state etc.

Those who wrote a general essay without reference to the sources would not gain many more than half marks. Similarly, those who merely paraphrased the sources with no outside knowledge or contextual awareness would not rise above half marks.

■ ■ ■

A-grade answer to question 1

(a) The 'communist acts of violence' specifically refers to the Reichstag fire. While the Nazi vote in the Reichstag election had declined from July to November 1932, the vote for the communists had continued to rise. It was partly the fear of a communist attempt to seize power that led President Hindenburg to appoint Hitler as Chancellor in January 1933. Immediately on his appointment, Hitler called new Reichstag elections and the 'communist threat' became the main theme of Nazi propaganda. The Nazi image of the 'national uprising' specifically targeted communists and socialists. In the middle of the election campaign the Reichstag was set alight and the communists were blamed. These 'communist acts of violence' allowed the Nazis to claim the need for a state of emergency to guard against the communist threat. This provided the justification for the Reichstag Fire Decree, which is outlined in Source A. This decree, which effectively suspended civil liberties, became the basis of Hitler's dictatorship throughout the Third Reich.

> The question requires a good understanding of the circumstances and events of the weeks after Hitler's appointment as Chancellor. The answer makes specific reference to the Reichstag Fire Decree and places the perceived communist threat in the context of the election campaign.

(b) In Source B Hitler is anxious to achieve powers of dictatorship by a 'legal' revolution, which would involve changing the constitution. Hitler's position on his appointment as Chancellor was not as strong as he would want. While President Hindenburg was still alive and while other political parties continued to exist, he would face potential opposition in his aim to achieve total power. However, he was aware that he owed his appointment as Chancellor to the traditional members of the conservative élite in politics and society. It was very important for him to reassure the leaders of the civil service, big industry, the armed forces and conservative politicians that he was 'safe' and respectable. He also had to reassure opinion in other European countries that he was not a dangerous revolutionary.

This move towards 'respectability' and the 'legal revolution' contrasted strongly with the aims of some of the SA stormtroopers, whose views were expressed by their leader Ernst Röhm in Source C. Röhm resented and was suspicious of Hitler's 'deals' struck with conservative politicians. 'The course of events between 30 January and 21 March' refers to Hitler's appointment as Chancellor and the 'Day of Potsdam', where Hitler publicly associated himself with the forces of tradition, respectability and the German Army. As strongly implied in the source, Röhm's aim was to sweep away the old order and achieve a full 'National Socialist revolution'. For Röhm, the events of February and March 1933 marked the beginning, not the end, of the 'revolution'. A 'second revolution' was needed against the forces of tradition and order, as Röhm threatens at the end of the passage.

Clearly, the two passages present two conflicting sets of objectives. The 'brown trash' of the SA, hated and feared by the traditional élites, were to prove a constant embarrassment and increasing threat to Hitler's 'legal revolution' until the situation was finally settled by the Night of the Long Knives in June 1934.

> This answer adequately considers and points out the fundamental differences between Röhm and Hitler on the question of 'revolution'. Outside knowledge is

used to explain not just the obvious differences in the passages but the *reasons* why they differ. The respective positions of Röhm and Hitler are explained briefly but clearly. There is accurate detailed reference to the appointment of Hitler and the Day of Potsdam. The focus on the actual question is clear and sharp, and this response adequately answers it.

(c) Since his failed attempt to seize power by force in Munich in 1923, Hitler had realised that power could not be achieved by violent means against the forces of law and order. Thus the NSDAP competed for votes in the Reichstag elections with the aim of becoming the largest party in Parliament. Hitler then used his position as leader of the largest party in the negotiations with von Papen and Hindenburg that led to his appointment as Chancellor in January 1933.

Hitler owed his position as Chancellor to the traditional conservative leaders who thought they had 'hired' him to destroy the communists and restore law and order to German society. They wrongly thought that once Hitler had done this he could be dispensed with. Hitler realised that in order to consolidate his power and achieve the one-party dictatorship with him as 'Führer' of the German nation, he must continue to rely on the traditional forces that had put him in power. Everything he did in the months following his appointment must be seen to be 'legal' and 'constitutional'.

Source A, the Reichstag Fire Decree, was issued within hours of the burning down of the Reichstag in a suspected communist plot. The 'restrictions on personal liberty' and the 'right of free expression of opinion and the right of assembly and association' formed the basis of a dictatorship that was to last until 1945. The justification for this was that there was a 'state of emergency' after the 'communist acts of violence'. There was nothing technically illegal about this. Article 48 of the Weimar Constitution provided for dictatorial powers to be used in a state of emergency. The Reichstag Fire Decree was issued by this authority, as stated in the source.

In order to remove the Reichstag as an independent institution, Hitler needed to change the constitution 'legally'. This would require a two-thirds majority in the Reichstag to achieve an enabling law. Source B, the minutes of a Cabinet meeting, shows Hitler attempting to persuade the Cabinet of the need for such a law. The majority of the Cabinet at this time were still non-Nazis, mainly conservatives. Therefore, again, Hitler had to appear to be 'legal' and 'correct'. As Hitler pointed out, the communists who would obviously have voted against the Enabling Bill would not appear in the Reichstag because they had been lawfully banned under the Reichstag Fire Decree.

The alternative to achieving total power by 'legal' means was the use of force and violence. This was strongly implied by Ernst Röhm, leader of the SA, in Source C. In the source he talks of 'revolution', using the word 'struggle'. Clearly, this was a threat to the forces of law and order and the security of the state and was in direct contrast to Hitler's 'legal' path. Hitler's dilemma was that if he allowed Röhm and his stormtroopers to act violently on the streets, the more conservative forces in society — big business, the Army leadership — on whom Hitler relied would put pressure on him to make up his mind. This meant either siding with the 'legal' forces and destroying the SA leadership or staying loyal to his old comrade Röhm and undertaking the 'full National Socialist revolution' that Röhm spoke of. By 1934 Hitler also knew that the President, Hindenburg, would not live much longer. He would need the support of the Army in order 'lawfully' to assume total power by combining the offices of President and Chancellor after Hindenburg's death. Clearly, therefore, Hitler would continue with the legal path and this issue was finally resolved in the Night of the Long Knives in June 1934. A few weeks later, after Hindenburg died, Hitler was able to secure an oath of allegiance from all members of the armed forces to him personally as Führer.

The violence of the Night of the Long Knives was explained by Hitler on 3 July 1934 in Source D. Hitler had just authorised mass murder and could be seen to have acted illegally. The important point is that Hitler was able to justify this by reference to the Reichstag Fire Decree mentioned in Source A. There had been a 'state of emergency' and the 'self-defence of the state' was necessary.

The destruction of the SA leadership 'in the interests of the state' was therefore 'legitimised' and removed the last obstacle in preparing the way for Hitler to succeed Hindenburg by 'lawful' means. As these sources show, this was all achieved by 'legal' or at least 'semi-legal' means.

> This answer focuses well on the question of legality, with a brief explanation at the beginning of why Hitler needed to consolidate his power by 'legal' means. The focus on the question of 'legal' or 'semi-legal' is sharp and persistent. There are detailed references to each of the sources in the light of the question, which go beyond simple paraphrasing. Overall, this is an impressive A-grade response which convincingly combines contextual knowledge with the passages.

The Nazi system of government

(a) **Study Source D**
From this source and your own knowledge, explain the reference to 'this witches' cauldron of struggles for position and conflicts over competence'. (20 marks)

(b) **Study Sources B and C**
Using your own knowledge, to what extent do the comments of Weidemann in Source C support the view put forward by Lammers in Source B? (40 marks)

(c) **Using all the sources**
From your own knowledge and these sources, discuss the view that Hitler was a 'weak dictator'. (60 marks)

Source A: *Postwar reflections of the constitutional lawyer Carl Schmitt, and State Secretary Carl von Weizsacker*

Hitler's personal position of power involved an immense claim to omnipotence but also the claim to omniscience. His omnipotence existed to a large extent in fact and was highly effective. His omniscience, however, was purely fictitious. The first practical question therefore was who conveyed to the omnipotent Führer the material on which his decisions were based and who selected from the mass of mail which arrived and decided what or was not to be shown to him? The second question concerned the other aspect of dealing with things, the passing on of orders and decisions to the executive, a question of special importance because there were no clearly defined forms for the so-called Führer orders and the orders were often brief and abrupt.

Source B: *Diary extract of the Lord Mayor of Hamburg in 1937 after a conversation with Heinrich Lammers, the head of the Reich Chancellery*

I had a long talk with State Secretary Lammers about Schacht. He said the Führer found it so difficult to make decisions about personnel. He always hoped that things would sort themselves out on their own. A decision has not yet been made because the Führer was not satisfied with the nomination of only one state secretary and would prefer to appoint a minister. He kept hoping that the question of personnel would solve itself. He, Lammers, had proposed the appointment of super ministers to whom some of the ministers would be subordinated as far as particular issues were concerned. The reason was that he found it extremely difficult to work with this large cabinet.

question

Source C: *Postwar comments of Fritz Weidemann, one of Hitler's adjutants on Hitler's working habits*

In 1935 Hitler kept to a reasonably ordered daily routine....Gradually, this fairly orderly work routine broke down. Later Hitler normally appeared shortly before lunch, quickly read through Reich Press Chief Dietrich's press cuttings, and then went into lunch. So it became more and more difficult for Lammers and Meissner to get him to make decisions which he alone could make as Head of State....When Hitler stayed at the Obersalzberg it was even worse. There he never left his room before 2 p.m. Then he went straight to lunch. He spent most afternoons taking a walk, in the evening, straight after dinner there were films....He disliked the study of documents. I have sometimes secured decisions from him, even ones about important matters, without his ever asking to see the relevant files. He took the view that many things sorted themselves out on their own if one did not interfere.

Source D: *Otto Dietrich commenting on the personal rivalries and overlapping jurisdictions of the various agencies which developed in the Nazi political system*

It was not laziness or an excessive degree of tolerance which led to the otherwise so energetic and forceful Hitler to tolerate this witches' cauldron of struggles for position and conflicts over competence. It was intentional. With this technique he systematically disorganised the upper echelons of the Reich leadership in order to develop and further the authority of his own will until it became a despotic tyranny.

Mark scheme

(a) Comprehension of a source

To gain a mark in the higher band you would have to show a clear understanding of the tendency for big 'empires' to develop as a consequence of the Nazi political system and Hitler's style of leadership. Good answers might identify examples of 'conflicts over competence', e.g. the question of who, if anybody, had ultimate responsibility for education, the economy etc. Better answers might refer to the information given in the other passages. You would not be expected to explain why this situation arose, but those who explained briefly that this could be seen as a natural consequence of the workings of the Nazi political system would be rewarded.

(b) Comparison of two sources

The better answers would reveal a good working knowledge of both Hitler's own working habits and the ways in which the Nazi political system operated. Again, you would benefit by using your own knowledge in conjunction with the information given in the two extracts. For example, to what extent does the image portrayed by Weidemann in C support the view of the procrastinating and indecisive leader

OCR Unit 1

portrayed by Lammers in B? At the higher end, the examiner could expect comments about Hitler's aversion to paperwork, his boredom with the routine business of government, his concentration on the 'grand visions', his view of himself as an 'artist' and 'romantic' who was above political and governmental decisions. Answers that concentrated exclusively on the information in the two sources would not go beyond half marks.

(c) Judgement in context, based on a set of sources and own knowledge

At the higher end, you would be expected to refer to all the sources in conjunction with a wider knowledge of the topic. Credit would be given to those who pointed out the differences between the *theory* of Hitler's (omnipotent) power and the limitations of that power in practice. There are many clues in the given extracts. For example, Hitler could only know what was preselected for him to see (Source A). Source B gives the impression of a weak and indecisive leader. Source C, when used in conjunction with outside knowledge, could shed some light on the question of whether Hitler was a 'weak dictator'. Source D offers a particular viewpoint that the perceptive and knowledgeable candidate might challenge. Straightforward paraphrasing of the given extracts without clear use of outside knowledge would not score much above half marks.

■ ■ ■

A-grade answer to question 2

(a) Hitler saw himself as standing above politics. He was the Führer of the German nation. He claimed to represent the 'nation's will'. He was also bored by the routine business of government. Reluctant to commit himself in writing, he was preoccupied with the 'grand design'. The precise methods by which this 'design' were to be achieved were left to the various Nazi leaders to work out. As a result of this, the Nazi political system developed into a bitter struggle between rival 'empires' to gain influence and prestige with the Führer. This is what Dietrich meant by a 'witches' cauldron of struggles for position' in Source D. Another consequence of Hitler's style of leadership was the lack of clear-cut areas of competence and jurisdiction between the various ministries and government departments. For example, the vital issue of education was a concern not just for the Education Ministry but also for the Propaganda Ministry, the SS, the German Labour Front (DAF) and the Hitler Youth. With such overlapping jurisdictions and confusions over who was ultimately responsible for what, it is not surprising that, as Dietrich says, the 'upper echelons of the Reich leadership' were disorganised. The reflections on Hitler's lifestyle and working habits shown in Source C will help to explain why this situation developed.

> In this answer, both aspects of the question are adequately dealt with. The reasons why there was rivalry between leading Nazi figures are clearly explained with a brief discussion of Hitler's working style. Examples from outside knowledge

AS History

question

are given to illustrate the overlapping jurisdictions and confusions which arose from the 'conflicts over competence'. There is also a useful cross-reference with Source C.

(b) In Source C Fritz Weidemann describes Hitler's extraordinarily lazy lifestyle and working routine. The impression given is of a leader who avoided wherever possible the need to address the important governmental issues of the day. This contrasts strongly with the traditional image of a firm and decisive leader. The statement that 'he took the view that many things sorted themselves out on their own if one did not interfere' strongly supports the impression given by Lammers in Source B.

The laziness implied in Source C would also go some way to explaining Hitler's tendency to create new, overlapping ministries and departments rather than replace the existing ones which Lammers talks about in Source B. Hitler's difficulty in making decisions about personnel mentioned by Lammers is strongly supported by Weidemann's view that it was increasingly difficult for Lammers and others to get important decisions from Hitler.

Both sources give the impression of a leader who shut himself away from reality, both physically and mentally. Much of the time Hitler would be in the Obersalzberg in the Bavarian mountains, a long way from the realities he would have to face in the capital, Berlin. The rather solitary lifestyle described by Weidemann, the long walks, lunching alone, also tends to support the impression given by Lammers that Hitler was uncomfortable when dealing with large bodies of people. Indeed, the Cabinet did not meet formally after 1937.

The two sources complement each other. The lazy lifestyle, dislike of paper-work, indecisiveness and procrastination described in Source C go a long way to explaining the image portrayed by Lammers in Source B.

> The answer points out that the two sources largely complement each other. Both passages consider Hitler's working style. A good working knowledge of the operation of the Nazi political system is used to amplify and illustrate the similarities. This is a good example of the passages being put into the wider context of the topic.

(c) In contrast to the traditional view that the political system of the Third Reich functioned smoothly with a clear chain of command from the top downwards, and that the Führer was the all-powerful decisive leader, historians such as Hans Mommsen and Martin Broszat have created a picture of a rather weak and indecisive leader who presided over a system of 'organised chaos'.

There is plenty of evidence in the given extracts to suggest that the Nazi political system was riddled with confusions and that Hitler did not and could not be fully aware of what was done in his name. The basis of his power, the theoretical justification for it, was that he was leader because of his own extraordinary 'charismatic' qualities. His position was therefore defined in vague terms. Clearly, he was a dictator in theory, since there were no legal channels in the machinery of government that could provide for any limitations on his power. He could thus claim to be 'omnipotent', as described in Source A. However, as Schmitt and Weizsacker state, the information on which Hitler could base his decisions was preselected for him by others. The implication is that Hitler was shown only what he might want to see and that much important information was concealed from him. As implied in the source, those who did the 'preselecting' were themselves in very important positions of power. Hitler obviously could therefore never be 'all-knowing'. Depending on information selected for him by others, he could hardly act as an all-powerful dictator.

If one assumes that an important characteristic of a strong dictator is decisiveness and firmness and clarity in decision making, then the impression given in both Sources B and C, of procrastination, indecisiveness and laziness, would suggest the image of a 'weak dictator'. If Lammers is correct in Source B, a leader who 'hoped that things would sort themselves out' implies a kind of weakness, an unwillingness to face decisions and make up his mind.

Hitler's lifestyle and working habits as described in Source C suggest that Hitler shut himself away from reality, leaving important decisions to others. His dislike of the study of documents and paperwork, his rather solitary lifestyle and his uneasiness when faced with large groups of ministers, meant that orders from above were often verbally issued by the Führer, sometimes in casual conversation. With so few clear, written orders from above, it became a matter of 'interpreting' the 'Führer's will', or 'working towards the Führer'. Obviously, this system of issuing and carrying out orders was open to abuse and distortion.

The 'witches' cauldron of struggles for position and conflicts over competence' described by Otto Dietrich in Source D suggests that as a consequence of Hitler's style, great 'empires' developed within the political system, rivalling each other and struggling for superiority. The biggest 'empire' of all was that of the SS under Heinrich Himmler which, by the time of the Nazi occupation of eastern Europe during the war, controlled the concentration camp system and was influential in administering the occupied territories. With Hitler's increasing tendency to shut himself away from reality and the outside world, it is not surprising that some historians have claimed that the real power lay with Himmler and the SS. However, despite the impression of weakness implied by Dietrich, he actually states that the confusion and rivalries were intentionally created by Hitler in order to 'divide and rule', on the assumption that if Nazi leaders were at each others' throats they were unlikely to group together to challenge the Führer's power.

In conclusion, Hitler's position as dictator can be seen in two ways. In theory, his power was all-embracing and his ministers and government officials were authorised to 'interpret his will'. In practice, however, his indecisiveness, remoteness and tendency to leave important things to others strongly suggests

AS History

weakness. The alternative opinion to Dietrich's in Source D is that the confusions and rivalries developed as a consequence of Hitler's leadership style and were increasingly outside his control. The impression given by the other sources would seem to support this and suggest that Hitler was in fact a 'weak dictator'.

> Here, the focus on 'weak dictator' is kept to the fore. The important point about the difference between the theory and the actuality of Hitler's power is convincingly illustrated. Relevant aspects of each of the passages are illustrated and amplified by a good use of outside knowledge. The mini-essay leads to a sensible and logical conclusion.

Opposition to Hitler

(a) **Study Source A**
   From this source and your own knowledge, explain 'the new government no longer intends to leave the people to their own devices'. (20 marks)

(b) **Study Sources A and D**
   Compare the views expressed in Source D with the aims set out in Source A and explain the differences. (40 marks)

(c) **Using all the sources**
   From your own knowledge and these sources, discuss the view that open opposition to the Nazi regime failed because the majority of the German population *passively* tolerated the Nazis. (60 marks)

Source A: Goebbels outlining his view of the role of the Reich Ministry of Popular Enlightenment and Propaganda, March 1933

I see in the setting up of the new Ministry of Popular Enlightenment and Propaganda by the government a revolutionary act in so far as the new government no longer intends to leave the people to their own devices. This government is in the truest sense of the word a people's government. It arose out of the people and will always execute the will of the people....We want to give the people their due, though admittedly in another form than occurred under parliamentary democracy. In the newly formed ministry...I envisage the link between regime and people, the living contact between the national government, as the expression of the people's will, and the people themselves....It is not enough for people to be more or less reconciled to our regime, to be persuaded to adopt a neutral attitude towards us, rather we want to work on people until they have capitulated to us, until they grasp ideologically that what is happening in Germany today not only *must* be accepted but also *can* be accepted.

Source B: An SPD (Social Democratic Party) report on popular attitudes to Hitler following the Night of the Long Knives

Our reports show that the events of 30 June have not shaken the authority of Hitler in the SA and the Party but that his authority among the people has, if anything, grown. He's got more guts; he takes tough action; he does not spare the bigwigs — those were the remarks made even by outsiders. Wherever in Germany people grumble about the maladministration, about the brown big-shots, Hitler is normally excepted. He does not want all that and is simply badly advised and informed. This effect of Hitler on the indifferent masses also extends to the workers in so far as they are not politically educated. Our factory reports record cases in which during factory visits Hitler undoubtedly has an effect on workers as well.

question

Source C: An SPD report from central Germany in 1936

The average worker is primarily interested in work and not in democracy. People who previously enthusiastically supported democracy show no interest at all in politics. One must be clear about the fact that in the first instance men are fathers of families and have jobs, and that for them politics take second place and even then only when they expect to get something out of it.

Many people reject participation in illegal activity on account of this basic attitude. They consider it pointless and that one only ends up in jail because of it. But that does not by any means imply that they are going over to the Nazis.

Source D: A report of the Military Economic Inspectorate on reactions to the Munich crisis of September 1938

There was great tension and concern everywhere and people expressed the wish that there should be no war. This was put particularly firmly by the front-line fighters of the World War....Listening to foreign broadcasts has produced confusion and fickleness on the part of the great mass of the politically uneducated. Political indoctrination and education, particularly to prepare people for war, is still completely inadequate. Only very few of the lower-ranking Party leaders at present in office have achieved success with this education. One can only regard it as an almost total failure.

■ ■ ■

Mark scheme

(a) Comprehension of a source

To gain a mark in the higher band, reference should be made to the general propaganda aims of Goebbels and the Nazis. Credit would be given to those who understood that the Nazi aim was to guide, direct and control opinion in all its forms. Specific references to the control of the press, radio and the attempt to influence all forms of culture would be expected. There are some clues in the given extract, but those who merely paraphrased the extract without bringing in outside knowledge would receive, at best, half marks.

(b) Comparison of two sources

Source D indicates that the aims set out in Source A had not been achieved by 1938. To gain the higher marks, you would have to provide some reasons why. Very good responses might suggest that the bulk of the population saw much to admire and be happy about after 5 years of Nazism (the feeling of 'belonging', the eradication of the communist threat, provision of employment, foreign policy and diplomatic successes etc.), but ordinary Germans certainly did not want Germany to be embroiled in another European war. Such responses would indicate that a fundamental aim of Nazi propaganda was to prepare people physically and mentally for a future war, and while it could be argued that the majority were 'reconciled to our regime' (Source A), the larger aim of full 'totalitarian' indoctrination had yet to be achieved, as suggested in Source D.

(c) Judgement in context, based on a set of sources and own knowledge
Responses at the higher end would consider the notion of 'passive acceptance' in conjunction with the given extracts. For example, Source A implies the all-embracing efforts the regime would make in order to effect a thorough indoctrination. Source B strongly implies an almost ostrich-like desire to accept Hitler as a 'saviour' despite the growing unpopularity and distaste for the unsavoury activities of the 'Nazi bigwigs'. Source C offers a number of reasons why the average worker might 'turn a blind eye' to the unpleasant aspects: a mixture of fear and self-interest. Source D indicates the limits to which this passive acceptance might go (but the source does highlight the older generation, who fought in the trenches in 1914–18, rather than the younger generation, who were the chief targets of Nazi propaganda). Very good answers would pinpoint some of the reasons why the population might be willing to 'accept passively' the regime, and would use the information given in the extracts to support the points made. Those who wrote a general essay without reference to the sources would not go above half marks. Similarly, a mark of 30 would be the maximum for those who simply paraphrased the extracts without using outside knowledge to put the question in focus.

■ ■ ■

A-grade answer to question 3

(a) In Source A Goebbels is clearly setting out the totalitarian aims of the new Propaganda Ministry. This is indicated by the statement about 'leaving people to their own devices'. In other words, people must not be free to form opinions of their own. There should therefore be no free press and *all* forms of media (radio, the press, the arts, the cinema) must be controlled by the Nazi state. Opinion must be guided and directed. Within months of establishing the new ministry Goebbels had secured ultimate censorship over the national press. By 1939 the majority of Germans had access to a cheap radio. In the towns and cities, loudspeakers were installed in public areas and in factories and offices. The extent to which Goebbels aimed to control opinion is revealed in the statement 'we want to work on people until they have capitulated to us'. Thus, few Germans, particularly in urban areas, could escape the Nazi message.

> This answer clearly identifies the implications of the quotation referred to. It shows an understanding of the totalitarian aims of Nazi propaganda as set out by Goebbels in the passage. Examples of control of the various media are given and the answer supports the points made by quoting from the passage in a relevant fashion.

AS History

question 3

(b) In Source A, Goebbels is setting out the aims of Nazi propaganda on the establishment of his new ministry in 1933. These aims go far beyond simple 'reconciliation to the regime...until they (the people) have capitulated to us'. Through the use of radio, the press, the arts, cinema, mass rallies and education, the German people must become true Nazis. Among other things this meant that the population should be prepared both physically and mentally for a future war. They should be taught to believe totally in the superiority of the Aryan master race and must accept that the Nazi regime and the German people were one and the same thing. This is what Goebbels meant by 'I envisage the link between regime and people, the living contact between the national government...and the people themselves'. Although aimed at everybody, this propaganda was directed mainly at the young, the leaders of the future.

Source D, reporting on reactions to the Munich crisis in 1938, strongly suggests that many of these aims and objectives had not been achieved. The source admits that the majority of the people feared another war and were therefore not prepared for one. It admits also that people illegally listen to foreign radio broadcasts. Political indoctrination is seen as 'an almost total failure'. The source is from a report by an official government agency not directly linked with the Propaganda Ministry, and one can assume it contains a certain degree of objectivity.

It is commonly accepted by historians that the fear and lack of mental preparedness for war among ordinary people was as common in Germany as it was in Britain or France. While people were ready to accept the benefits of the regime (the jobs, entertainments, feeling of 'belonging'), this stopped some way short of embracing a willingness to go to war and shed blood. The Munich crisis, during which Europe stood on the brink of war, came only 20 years after the end of the 1914–18 war. As stated in the source, the 'front-line generation' in particular would not want to have to go through all that again.

The comparison of the two sources suggests that after 5 years Goebbels had only partly succeeded in his aims of full totalitarian indoctrination.

> *e* This answer makes an effective comparison of the two passages. It adopts the straightforward approach of testing the information given in Source D against the aims set out by Goebbels in Source A. In particular, in both cases, the inference drawn from the passage is amplified, developed and explained by use of outside knowledge. Not only does the answer point out the differences, it also explains *why* the sources differ.

(c) 'Passive toleration' of the Nazi regime suggests that few people were willing to stand out and criticise the regime openly. There was opposition during the peacetime years, mainly from the churches, and there were examples of resistance from the Army leadership in 1938 and during the war. All of this failed, however, for a variety of reasons, one of the most important being that the majority of Germans accepted and tolerated the regime despite its more unpleasant aspects.

The fact that the regime increasingly became a police dictatorship in the grip of the SS and the Gestapo, ruling by fear and terror, meant that there was a strong incentive for people to accept the regime and what it stood for, for fear of the consequences of doing otherwise. This police terror, combined with the type of thorough indoctrination described in Source A, was a powerful incentive for people to put up with the more unpleasant aspects of the regime, to accept the regime as long as they themselves were not directly threatened. It was far easier to 'go along' with the regime, to accept the ideology, when one was on the receiving end of constant pro-Nazi, pro-Hitler propaganda on street corners, on the radio and in the workplace. To a certain extent, Goebbels' aims in Source A — that Nazi ideology 'not only *must* be accepted but also *can* be accepted' — succeeded.

This is borne out by Source B, which suggests that Goebbels' propaganda about the Hitler myth was succeeding, even among the workers. Although the Nazi 'bigwigs' were disliked, people were almost blind in their devotion to Hitler. They would accept and tolerate the Nazi 'bosses' because they convinced themselves, or were convinced, that the Führer was above all that.

Source C gives the strongest indication that people accepted and tolerated the Nazis. The SPD report indicates self-interest and basic selfishness as a major reason why people accepted the regime. As long as workers had jobs and could look after their families, then they would not ask too many questions or voice any criticisms about the unpleasantness of the regime. As the source says, it was pointless risking this and receiving a jail sentence. The last sentence — 'But that does not…imply that they are going over to the Nazis' — strongly suggests passive rather than active participation in the regime.

Source D, an admission that many of the Nazi indoctrination aims had failed, indicates the limits to which passive acceptance might go. People would accept the regime and what it stood for, but did not want war. However, even here, the report mentions only 'tension and concern' over the Munich crisis, implying that the regime had failed to achieve *active* acceptance in its propaganda. It seems that people would register concern, would grumble, but do little more than that. In any case, immediately after the Munich Conference Hitler's popularity was at its peak. He was seen as the man who had saved Europe from war.

In such an atmosphere it was obviously difficult for opponents of the regime to act openly. Few people would be willing to risk their lives or livelihoods. People could always convince themselves, find excuses, 'turn a blind eye' or, as the historian Ian Kershaw put it, 'retreat into the private sphere'. Open opponents of the regime could be seen as dangerous 'outsiders' to be denounced to the Gestapo, often by their neighbours. With the vast majority of the population tolerating and 'putting up with' the regime, the best way to survive and flourish was to 'keep one's head below the parapet' — not come to the notice of the authorities in any way. That goes a long way towards explaining the failure of opposition.

e This answer focuses correctly on the question of 'passive toleration', and this is kept in the forefront. It offers reasons why the statement in the question might be correct or apt, using outside knowledge to emphasise the points. Having done this, the answer then considers each of the passages in the light of the statement. This is a good example of the use of knowledge and a thorough reading of the sources to answer the question. In each passage, the response goes some way beyond simple paraphrasing. For example, in reference to Source C the answer develops and explains, using knowledge, the implications of the SPD man's report.

Nazi anti-Semitism

(a) **Study Source B**
   From this source and your own knowledge, explain what is meant by the 'Jewish laws' and 'to provide the SA with something to do'. (20 marks)

(b) **Study Sources C and D**
   Using your own knowledge, explain the extent to which the information in Source D supports that in Source C, and the extent to which it contradicts it. (40 marks)

(c) **Using all the sources**
   From your own knowledge and these sources, discuss the view that the Nazi persecution of the Jews in the 1930s was part of an incoherent policy imposed by the Party on an unwilling population. (60 marks)

Source A: Order from Deputy Leader Rudolf Hess to party leaders, April 1935

While I can understand that all decent National Socialists oppose these new attempts by Jewry with utter indignation, I must warn them most urgently not to vent their feelings by acts of terror against individual Jews, as this can only result in bringing Party members into conflict with the political police who consist largely of Party members, and this will be welcomed by Jewry. The political police can in such cases only follow the strict instructions of the Führer in carrying out all measures for maintaining peace and order, so making it possible for the Führer to rebuke at any time allegations of atrocities and boycotts made by Jews abroad.

Source B: Report from an SPD (Social Democratic Party) contact man in Saxony, September 1935

The Jewish laws are not taken very seriously because the population has other problems on its mind and is mostly of the opinion that the whole fuss about the Jews is only being made to divert people's attention from other things and to provide the SA with something to do. But one must not imagine that the anti-Jewish agitation does not have the desired effect on many people. On the contrary, there are enough people who are influenced by the defamation of the Jews and regard the Jews as the originators of many bad things....But the vast majority of the population ignore this defamation of the Jews; they even demonstratively prefer to buy in Jewish department stores and adopt a really unfriendly attitude to the SA men on duty there.

AS History

question

Source C: *Secret report by the Nazi Supreme Court on the incidents of Kristallnacht, 9–10 November 1938*

On the evening of 9 November 1938, Reich Propaganda Director and party member Dr Goebbels told the party leaders assembled at a social evening in the old town hall in Munich that in the districts of Kurhessen and Magdeburg-Anhalt there had been anti-Jewish demonstrations, during which Jewish shops were demolished and synagogues were set on fire. The Führer, at Goebbels' suggestion, had decided that such demonstrations were not to be prepared or organised by the party, but neither were they to be discouraged if they originated spontaneously....The oral instructions of the Reich Propaganda Director were probably understood by all the party leaders present to mean that the party should not appear outwardly as the originator of the demonstrations but that in reality it should organise them and carry them out.

Source D: *Report from the American Consul in Leipzig on the events of Kristallnacht*

The shattering of shop windows, looting of stores and dwellings of Jews, which began in the early hours of 10 November 1938, was hailed subsequently in the Nazi press as a 'spontaneous wave of righteous indignation throughout Germany, as a result of the cowardly murder of Third Secretary von Rath in the German Embassy at Paris'. So far as a very high percentage of the German populace is concerned, a state of popular indignation that would spontaneously lead to such excesses can be considered as non-existent. On the contrary, in viewing the ruins and attendant measures employed, all of the local crowds observed were obviously benumbed over what had happened and aghast over the unprecedented fury of Nazi acts that had been or were taking place with bewildering rapidity throughout their city.

■ ■ ■

Mark scheme

(a) Comprehension of a source

Marks at the higher end would go to those who made reference to the Nuremberg Laws passed in September 1935. Those who pointed out that the SA had no officially defined role after the Night of the Long Knives, but was still a potentially dangerous pressure group of rank-and-file anti-Semitic activists, would be suitably rewarded. Very good responses might refer to the circumstances of the passing of the laws; the pressure put on Hitler and the leadership to pass some dramatic new anti-Semitic legislation. Those who referred only to one of the aspects in the question would gain a maximum of only half marks.

(b) Comparison of two sources

There are similarities and differences between the two sources and good answers would be expected to point these out both by referring to the sources and by using personal outside knowledge to support the points made. At the higher end, reference might be made to Goebbels' need to regain Hitler's favour by organising a 'spontaneous' mass demonstration of anti-Semitic feeling among the population. The extent to which this was actually 'spontaneous' might be gauged from Source D, although good answers might consider the provenance of this source. The highest marks would go to those who placed the events of Kristallnacht, and these conflicting interpretations, into the whole context of the relations between the regime and the Jews by 1938. Those who simply paraphrased the two extracts without use of outside knowledge would not go beyond half marks at best.

(c) Judgement in context, based on a set of sources and own knowledge
For marks in the highest band, both the questions of 'coherent policy' and 'unwilling population' would have to be addressed. There are plenty of clues in the sources. For example, Sources A and C both suggest the lack of a coherent policy either in 1935 or 1938. Sources B and D both imply an 'unwilling' population, although good answers would point out the qualifications to this in Source B. Source A also suggests that anti-Semitic violence was carried out by the party rank and file rather than ordinary members of the population. The best candidates would use the sources thoroughly in conjunction with their own knowledge to reach a sensible conclusion. Those who addressed only one of aspect of the question would achieve a maximum of half marks. Similarly, those who paraphrased the passages without use of outside knowledge could only be awarded a maximum of 30 marks.

A-grade answer to question 4

(a) The 'Jewish laws' referred to in the SPD report in Source B are the Nuremberg Laws of September 1935. By 1935 Hitler was under pressure from the rank-and-file members of the party to 'do something' about the Jews. Until now, anti-Semitic persecution had been largely confined to laws removing Jews from the main professions. Hitler and the leadership had to tread carefully in persecuting the Jews because of the need to achieve a 'respectable' image at home and abroad. This did not satisfy the more extreme anti-Semites of the rank and file, particularly the SA, who wanted dramatic and drastic action against the Jews, whatever the consequences, for Hitler's public image.

With the comment 'to provide the SA with something to do', the SPD man is referring to the fact that after the Night of the Long Knives of June 1934, where the SA leadership was destroyed, the SA stormtroopers had no clearly defined role. However, they continued to exist and were still a force within the party organisation that needed an 'outlet' for their aggression. It was very much 'pressure from below' that forced Hitler to announce the laws forbidding physical relations between Jews and non-Jews, which became the basis of the Nuremberg Laws.

AS History

question

> Both aspects of the question are addressed. There is a correct identification of the Nuremberg Laws and a brief explanation of how these laws came to be passed. This naturally links with a comment on the more violently anti-Semitic activities of the SA rank and file. This is a detailed, focused answer that deserves high marks for putting both aspects clearly into context.

(b) Sources C and D both refer to the events of Kristallnacht on 9–10 November 1938, during which Jewish shops were looted and hundreds of Jews were beaten up or murdered. After 5 years of power, the Nazis had progressively removed Jews from public life, beginning with laws against their participation in the professions, the Nuremberg Laws defining 'Jewishness' and forbidding physical contact between Jews and non-Jews, and with the SS leadership following a policy of Jewish emigration after 1936. This still did not satisfy the more extreme anti-Semitic members of the party.

The years 1937–38 saw a considerable 'radicalisation' of all aspects of the Nazi regime. By now Hitler's dictatorship had been consolidated and he was able to 'Nazify' the senior ranks of the civil service and the armed forces. With less need now for Hitler to be quite so concerned with foreign opinion, this period was very ominous for the German Jews.

It was in this context that Joseph Goebbels, who had fallen out of favour with Hitler over his affair with a Czech actress, seized upon the idea of a 'spontaneous' attack on the Jews by ordinary German people in order to impress and please Hitler. The image of ordinary German people spontaneously attacking and beating up Jews without direction from above would comply with Hitler's general propaganda line that he was representing and carrying out the wishes of his people.

Source C, the secret report by the Nazi Supreme Court, would seem to confirm this. Hitler is clearly giving the 'go-ahead' to this, but only if the anti-Jewish demonstrations appeared to be 'spontaneous', without open organisation from the party. In reality, the level of 'spontaneity' was very low; the whole business was effectively 'directed' by the party, as stated in the last sentence.

Source D reveals more differences from than similarities to the information in Source C. The American Consul in Leipzig clearly states that the level of 'spontaneity' was 'non-existent'. The fact that this came from an outsider referring only to one major city should be taken into account. He is reporting on the 'benumbed' state of the local crowds and would not at this time know the extent to which the whole thing was organised from above, since the report by the Supreme Court in Source C was secret. The source strongly implies that the violence was carried out against the knowledge and without the cooperation of the crowds, which does support what is implied in Source C.

> This answer reveals a good working knowledge of the background to and circumstances of Kristallnacht. It points out and explains the obvious differences but also considers aspects that are similar. The whole event is correctly placed in the

context of the 'radicalisation' of anti-Semitic policies during 1938. The answer shows a good mixture of paraphrasing and detailed knowledge.

(c) The Nazi Party did not have a blueprint planned in advance for dealing with the Jews once the Nazis were in power. Despite Hitler's rabble-rousing speeches and his violent anti-Semitic language, Hitler knew that he would have to cooperate with members of the traditional political élite in consolidating his dictatorship. He also had to present a reassuring image to foreign countries. Measures against the Jews would have to take a lower priority and would have to give the appearance of being 'legal'. The need to provide jobs, stabilise the economy and present a 'respectable' image were of higher priority initially. Also, many businesses were owned by Jews.

Thus, during 1933 and 1934, the leadership had to try to control the acts of violence committed against Jews by the party rank and file. Given that there was no coherent plan, often laws would be hurriedly rushed through after acts of violence against the Jews had taken place. Even the Nuremberg Laws, the most significant anti-Semitic laws of the 1930s, were only decided on by Hitler on the eve of the Nuremberg rally of 1935.

There is evidence in the sources to suggest that the Nazis had no coherent policy. Rudolf Hess in Source A reveals the lack of clear directions from above and the dilemma the leadership faced in trying to curtail the anti-Semitic violence coming from below. The impression given is of a situation getting out of control rather than the putting into practice of a coherent policy.

Sources C and D also imply that even 5 years later the party still had no coherent policy or clear guidelines. The whole dramatic episode of Kristallnacht only came about because of the murder of a German official in Paris 2 days before. Kristallnacht was more a consequence of Goebbels' poor relations with Hitler than part of a plan or a coherent policy.

The question of whether the majority of the German population were willing participants in anti-Semitic persecution is more difficult to assess. There were only half a million Jewish people living in Germany in 1933 and most of those lived in major cities like Berlin and Frankfurt. The overwhelming majority of Germans would rarely, if ever, have come into contact with Jews. Of course, many might have been persuaded by the crude anti-Semitic propaganda put out in the media and taught in the schools, but this does not necessarily mean that they would be willing to participate actively in street violence against the Jews, although it might help to explain the lack of a public outcry against the violence.

Source A, the order from Hess to party leaders, is referring only to the party rank and file, the implication being that it is the party members rather than ordinary citizens who are acting violently. The SPD report in Source B, although possibly biased against the regime, strongly suggests a kind of apathy, or certainly a lack

AS History

of willingness, of the inhabitants of Saxony to take the anti-Semitic laws very seriously. Indeed, many ignored the laws and continued to shop in Jewish stores in defiance of the authorities.

Goebbels' oral instructions in Source C, implying that the acts of violence should be organised by the party, again confirms the impression that anti-Semitic violence was imposed from above on an unwilling population. The American Consul in Leipzig also confirms this, the impression being that for the citizens of Leipzig, at least, the violence of Kristallnacht was shocking, unexpected and frightening.

The only clear pattern which emerges from the Nazi persecution of the Jews in the 1930s is that as the regime became stronger at home and more confident abroad, so the measures and actions against the Jews became more extreme and violent. As the sources suggest, these measures were imposed upon a largely reluctant population.

e Both aspects of the question are adequately addressed. 'Incoherent' implies a lack of a clear blueprint or any kind of planning. Building on the information supplied in earlier responses, the answer briefly considers examples of reactive rather than proactive Nazi anti-Semitic policies in the early years of the regime. Relevant passages are then referred to in support of this. The same approach is followed for the second aspect of the question. The whole answer has a clear focus, shows adequate knowledge of the topic and makes effective use of the sources.

C-grade answer to question 4

(a) The 'Jewish laws' means the laws the Nazis had passed against the Jews since 1933. The SPD man is saying that the population in Saxony are not taking the laws very seriously as they think this is a ruse by the government to divert attention from other things. However, there are some people who take the laws seriously because they are influenced by Nazi anti-Semitic propaganda.

'To provide the SA with something to do' refers to the fact that the SA men do not have proper jobs in the new government as they had hoped. They are beginning to feel surplus to requirements and the source says that some people even adopt an unfriendly attitude to the SA men on duty outside Jewish department stores.

(b) The information given by the American Consul in Source D largely agrees with the secret report by the Nazi Supreme Court in Source C. Source C talks about the aims of Goebbels, who wants to create the impression of a spontaneous attack against the Jews by ordinary Germans. Hitler said that demonstrations were not to be prepared or organised by the party but neither were they to be discouraged if they originated spontaneously. These are vague instructions which are interpreted by the party leaders to mean that in reality the party should organise the demonstrations.

This is backed up by Source D where the American Consul says that 'spontaneous activity' was probably non-existent. He talks of the 'benumbed' state of the local population after the night of violence. This suggests that the local population had little or nothing to do with the demonstrations and they were in fact organised by the party as suggested at the end of Source C.

However, the impression does contradict the Führer's suggestion in Source C that such demonstrations were not to be prepared or organised.

(c) Source A suggests that the Nazis had no coherent policy for dealing with the Jews in the early years of their power. Hess seems to be desperately trying to control the violent activities of the rank-and-file party members. He is not referring to ordinary members of the population, so the source implies that they had no part in the violence and so might be unwilling.

Source B says that the Jewish laws are not taken very seriously so this implies that the population was unwilling. The impression given by the source is that they didn't seem to care much either way; indeed, some of them adopt an unfriendly attitude to the SA men stationed outside Jewish department stores to stop people going in. The source doesn't really indicate whether attacks against the Jews were part of an incoherent policy.

Source C is ambiguous and slightly contradictory. It says that the demonstrations against the Jews should not be organised (according to Hitler), but later on it implies that in reality they should take place. If the demonstrations had to be organised by the party this would suggest that the population was unwilling. The fact that the source is ambiguous suggests that there was no clear or coherent government policy for dealing with the Jews.

Source D strongly suggests that the demonstrations were not welcomed by the local population. In fact they were 'benumbed' over the night of violence according to the American Consul. The fact that, as the source says, the shattering of shop windows, looting of stores and dwellings of Jews was a reaction against the 'cowardly murder of Third Secretary von Rath in the German Embassy at Paris' suggests that this was an unforeseen event and certainly not part of a coherent policy.

In conclusion, Sources A, C and D suggest that the Nazi policy against the Jews was incoherent. All the sources in one way or another suggest that this policy was foisted on an unwilling population.

This script would gain marks in the low C category. It is a good example of the paraphrase approach. In the answers to all of the sub-questions there is little use of outside knowledge: the candidate seems merely to have reworked what is in the passages. Some of this is done in a reasonably intelligent fashion, but what is lacking is an attempt to put the passages in their historical context, the fundamental skill required for high marks in this module.

AS History

The comparison of the passages in (b) simply refers to the texts without using knowledge to explain why they might agree or differ. The answer to (c) just trots through the sources, one by one, without any use of outside knowledge to explain their contents. There is some attempt to focus on the question, but the analysis is basic and doesn't go very far.

In addition, all the answers, particularly the one to question (c), are rather brief.